VINTAGE CHRISTMAS PHOTOS

Learning Specialist Bulletin, LLC

American Red Cross. "At the port of embarkation Army officers established a 'Christmas Box Hospital' for the repair of Christmas boxes received in the mails for shipment overseas to American soldiers in France." February 1918. Library of Congress. http://www.loc.gov/pictures/item/2017671907/

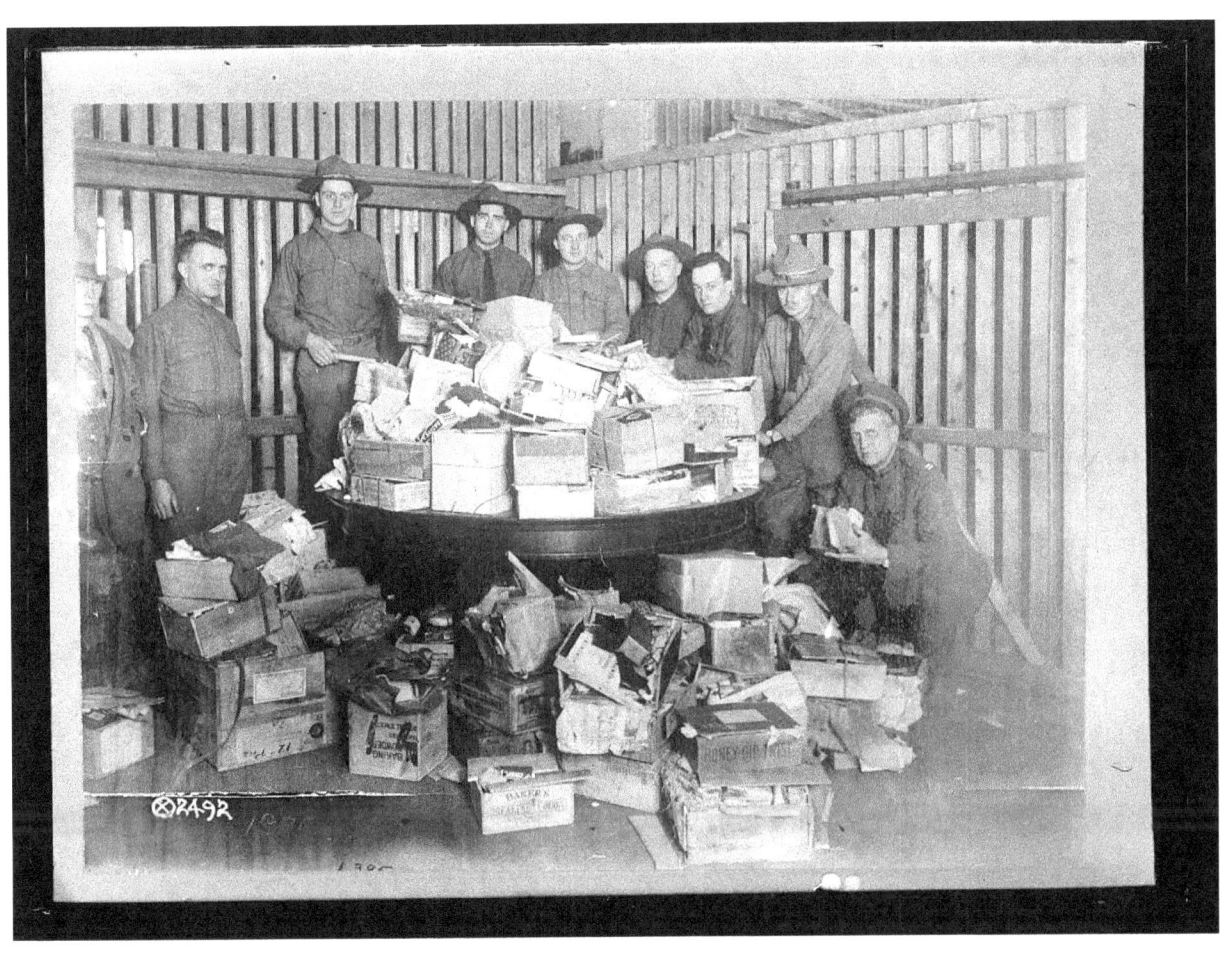

American Red Cross. "Christmas celebrations in the American Hospital in the London district. Santa Claus in the shell-shock ward." 5 December 1918. Library of Congress. http://www.loc.gov/pictures/item/2017676041/

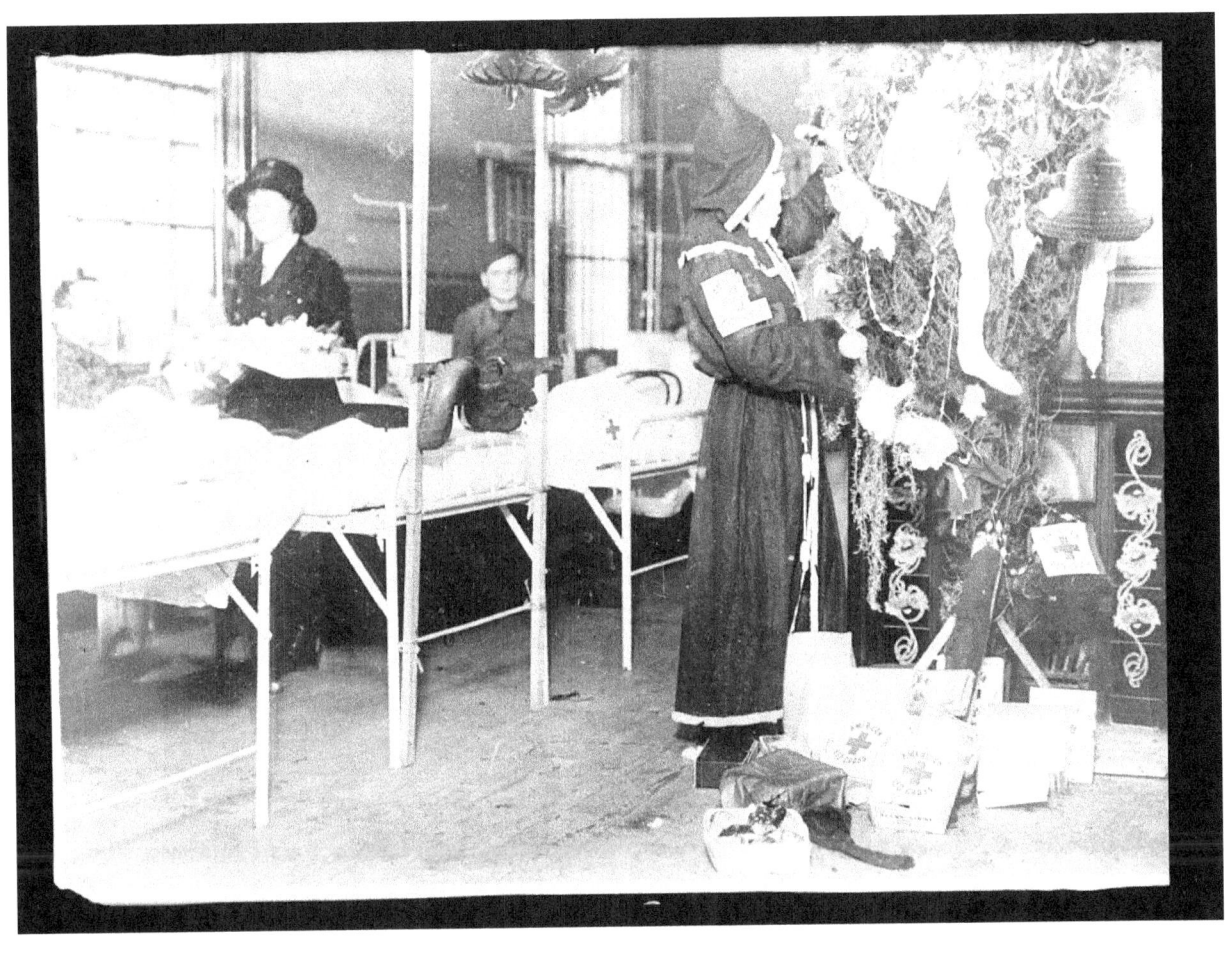

Diplomatic children send Christmas greetings. The children were from the France, Brazil, the United States, and Japan.

Harris & Ewing, photographer. "Diplomatic children broadcast Xmas greeting. Washington, D.C., Dec. 20." December 20, 1938. Library of Congress. http://www.loc.gov/pictures/item/2016874569/

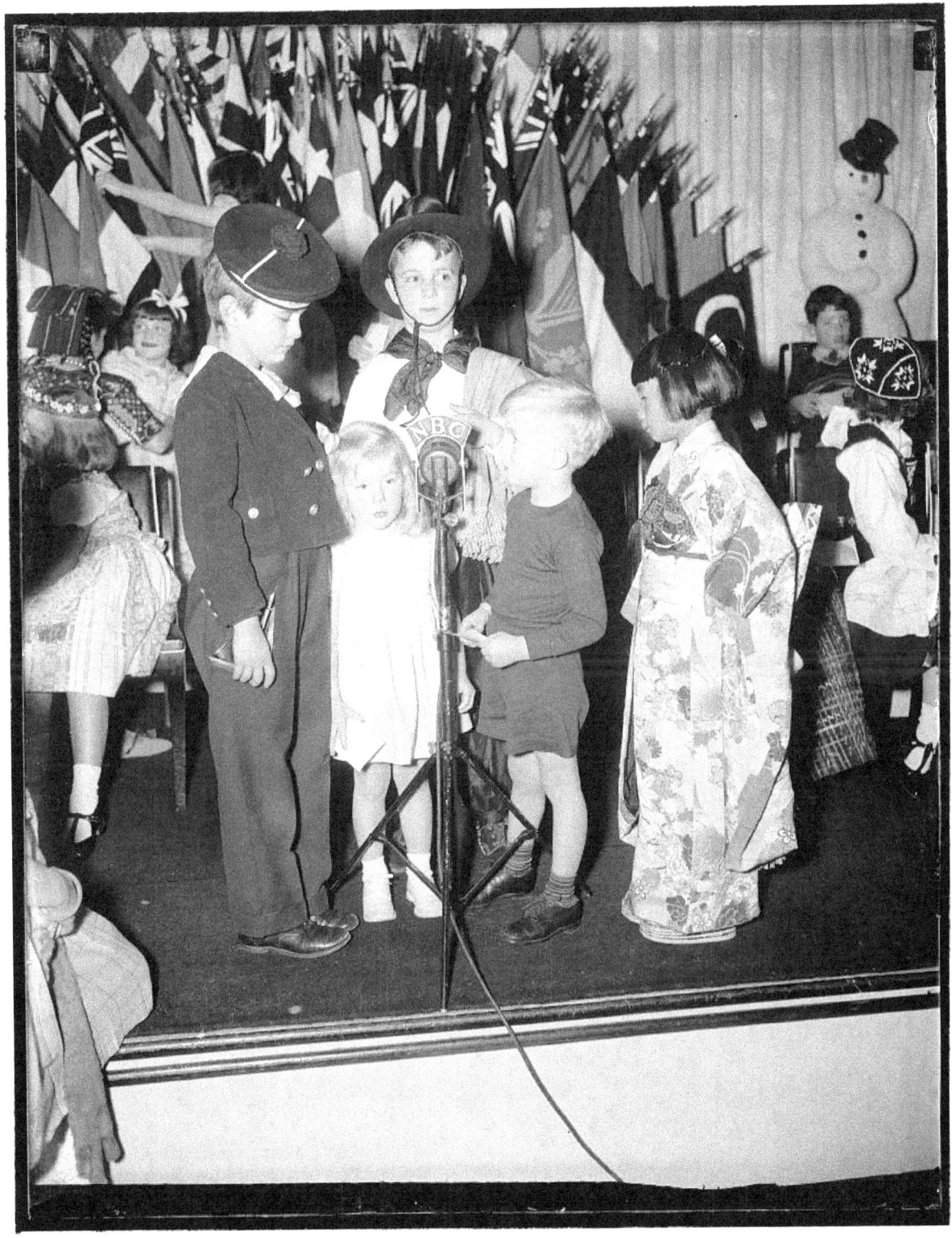

Harris & Ewing. "Christmas tree in East Room of White House. Washington, D.C., Dec. 23." December 23, 1936. Library of Congress. http://www.loc.gov/pictures/item/2016871018/

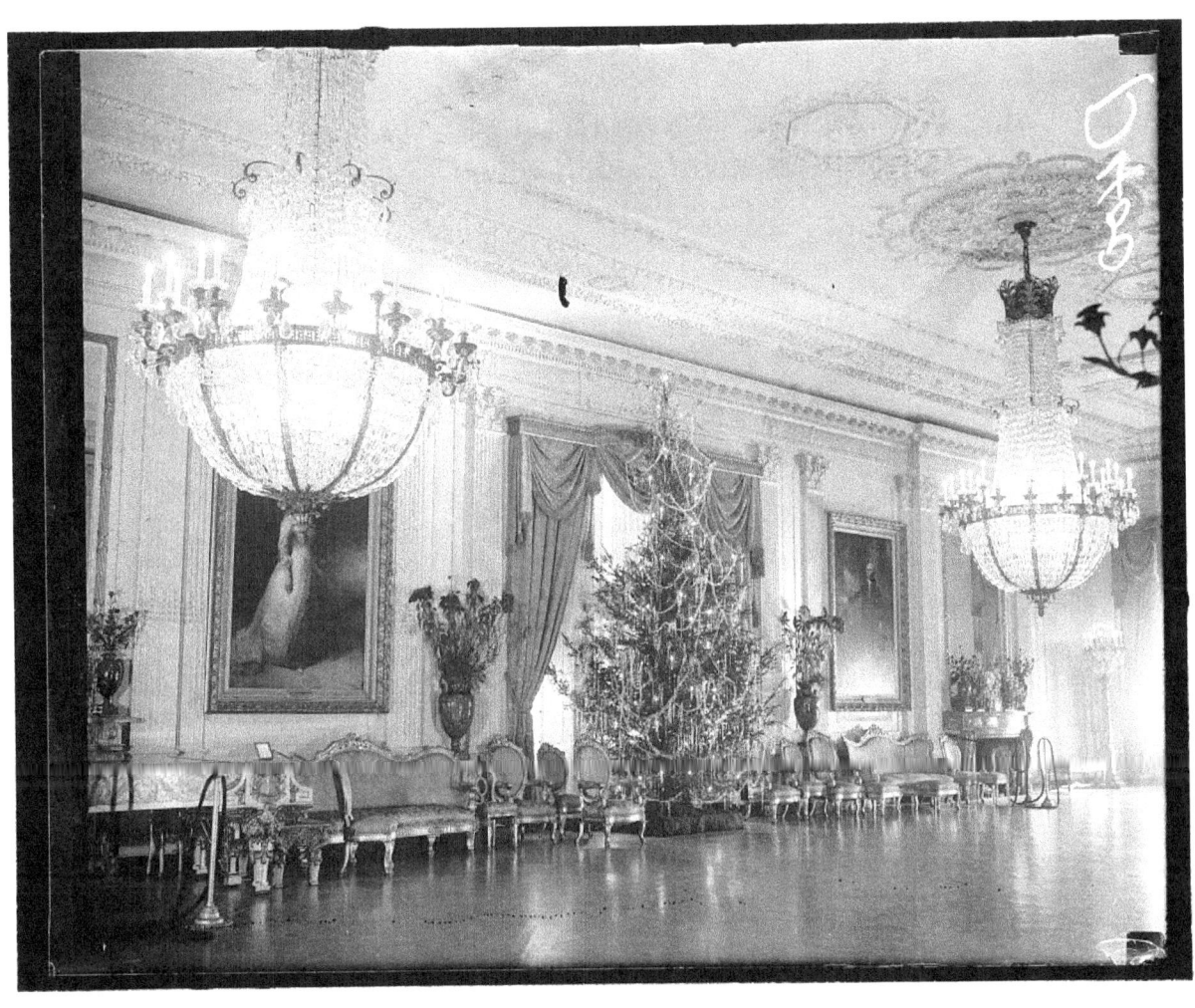

First Lady Eleanor Roosevelt looked at toys in a Washington, D.C., department store in 1934.

Harris & Ewing. "No Elephant Toys for First Lady." 1934. Library of Congress. http://www.loc.gov/pictures/item/2016883487/

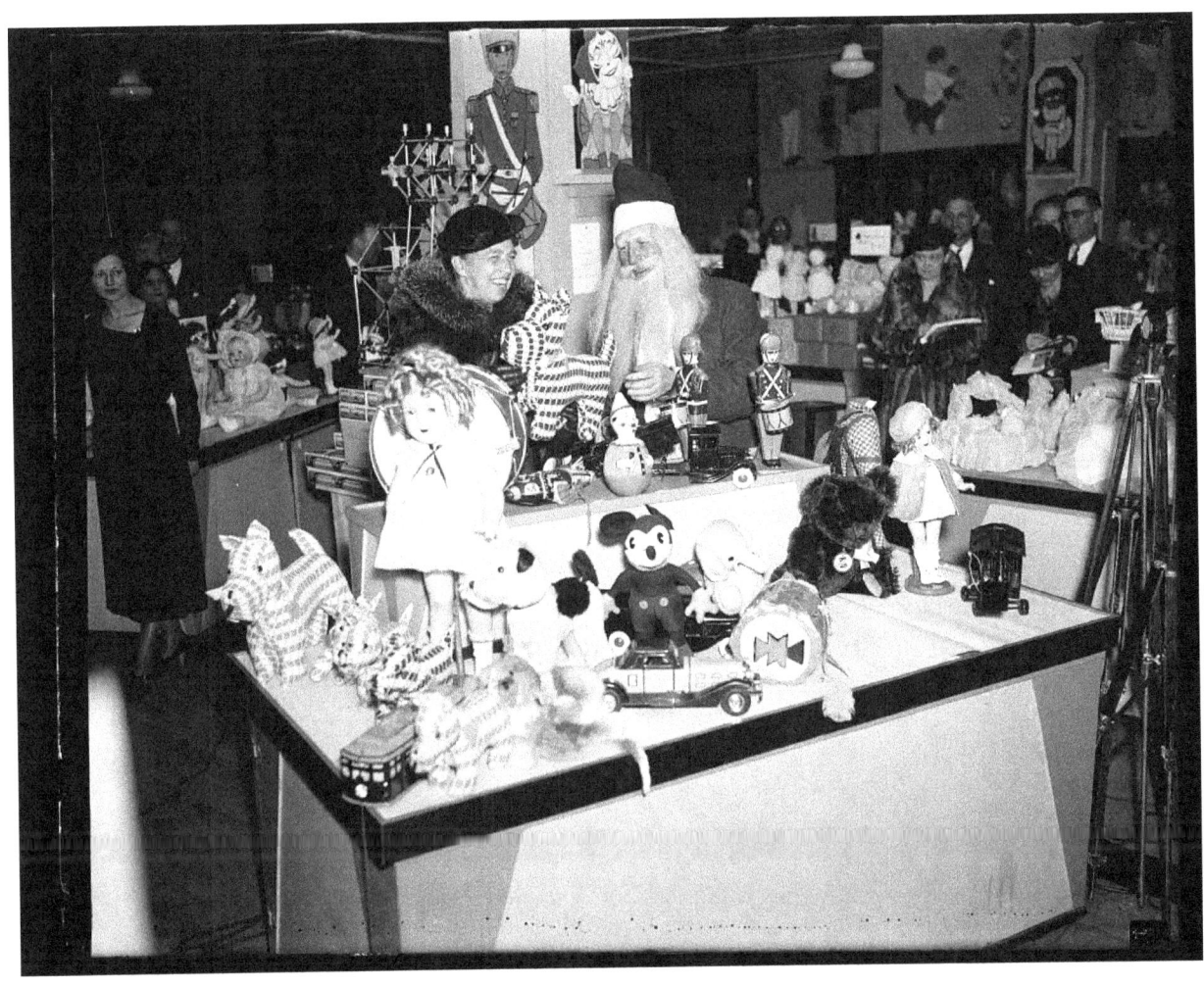

Harris & Ewing. "Santa Claus receives aeroplane pilot's license from Assistant Secretary of Commerce." November or December 1927. Library of Congress. http://www.loc.gov/pictures/item/2016888549/

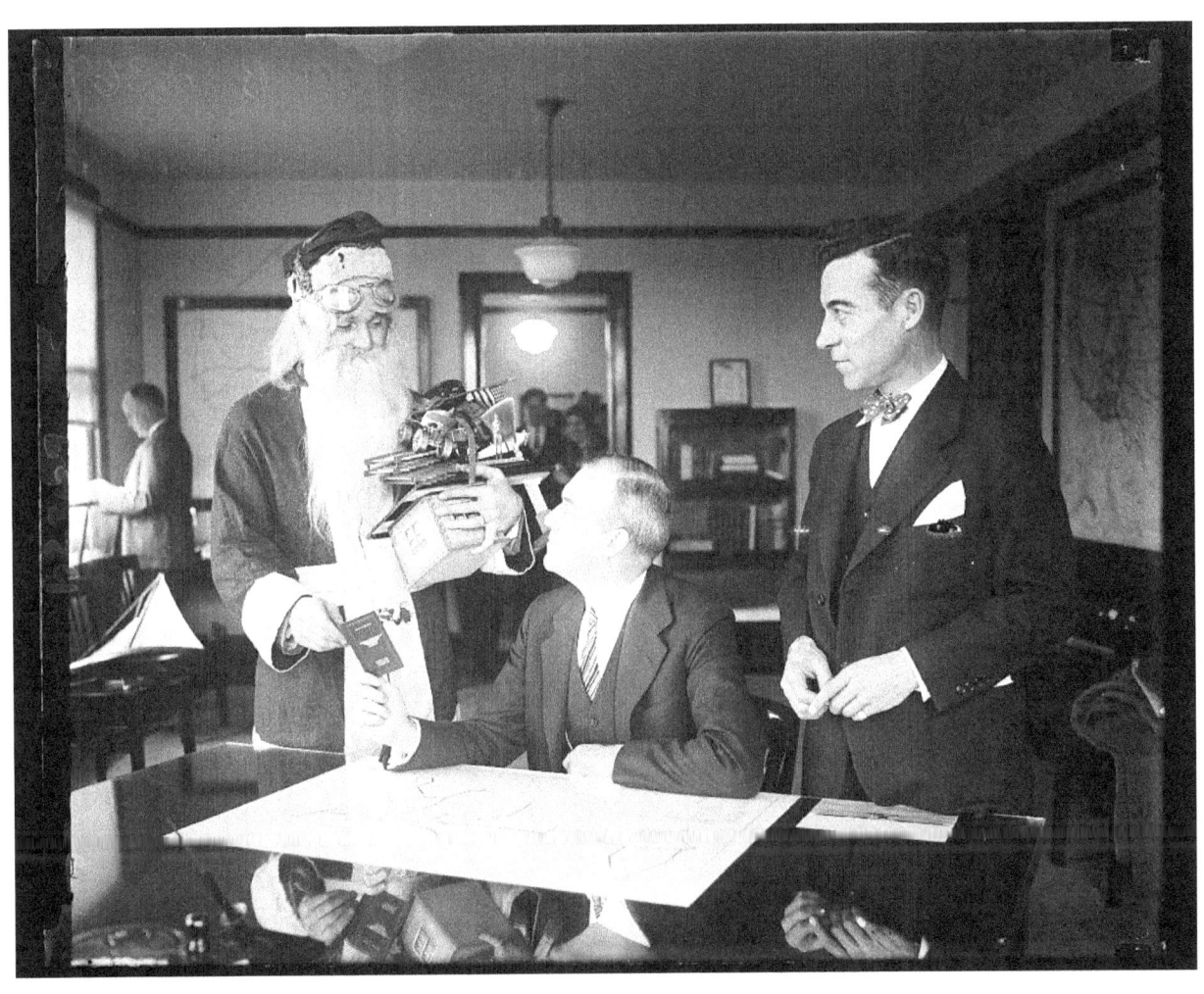

Wright, Wilbur and Orville. "Christmas Tree in the Wright Home, 7 Hawthorn Street, Dayton, Ohio." 1900. Library of Congress. http://www.loc.gov/pictures/item/2001696400/

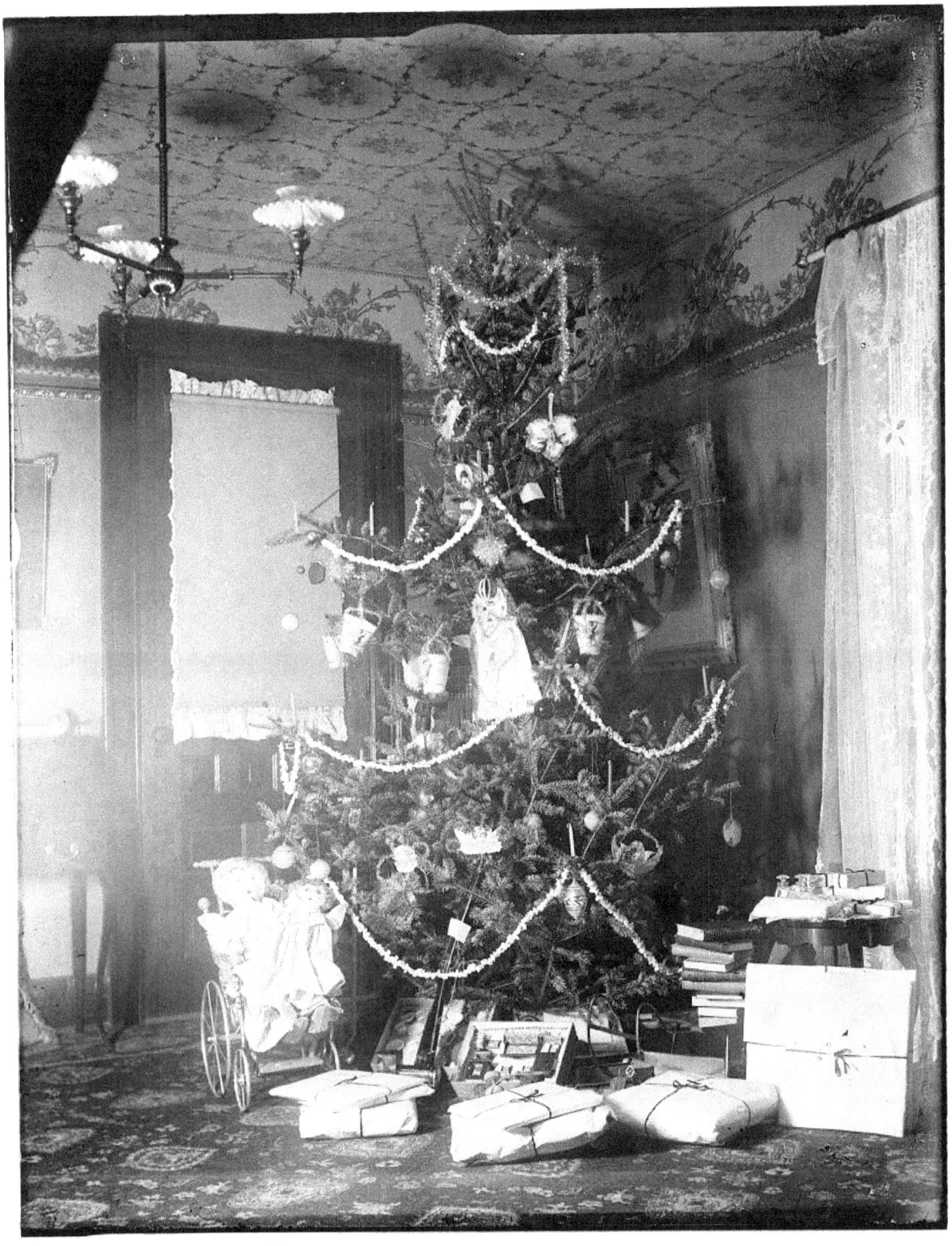

Underwood & Underwood, Publishers. "Lyndhurst--a Happy Christmas at 'Woody Crest.'" December 1905. Library of Congress. http://www.loc.gov/pictures/item/93507579/

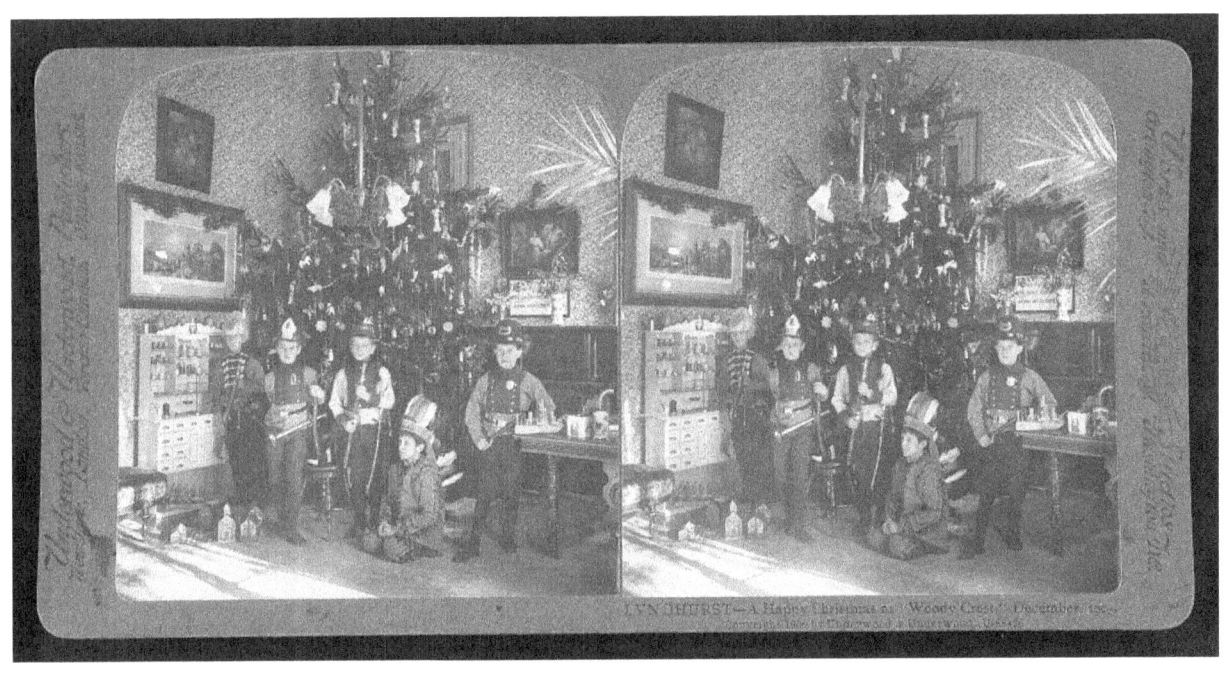

Collier, John, Jr. "Washington, D.C. Christmas Shopping in Woolworth's Five and Ten Cent Store." December 1941. Library of Congress. http://www.loc.gov/pictures/item/2017821811/

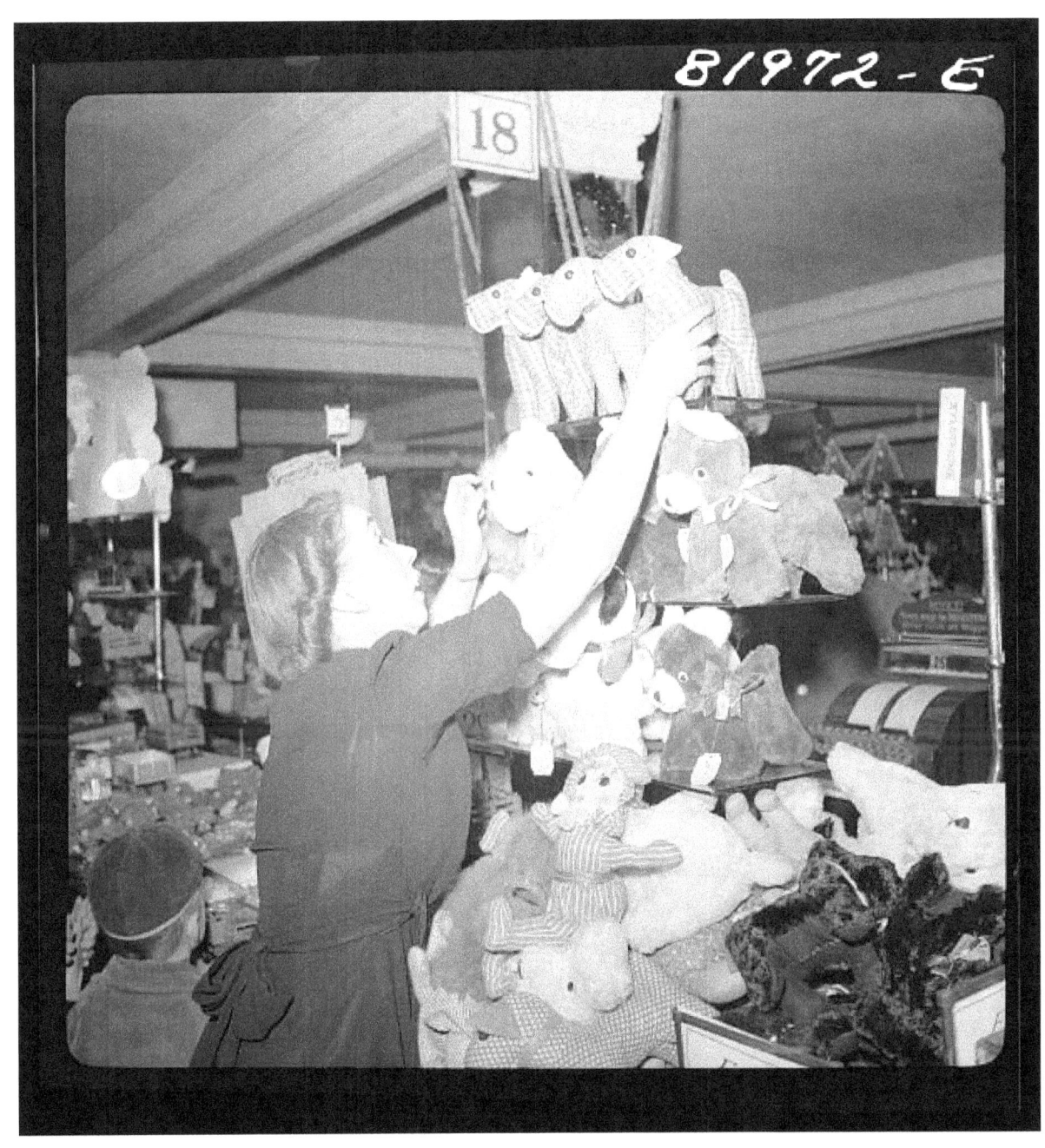

Collier, John., Jr. "Washington, D.C. Christmas in a home." December 1941. http://www.loc.gov/pictures/item/2017821860/

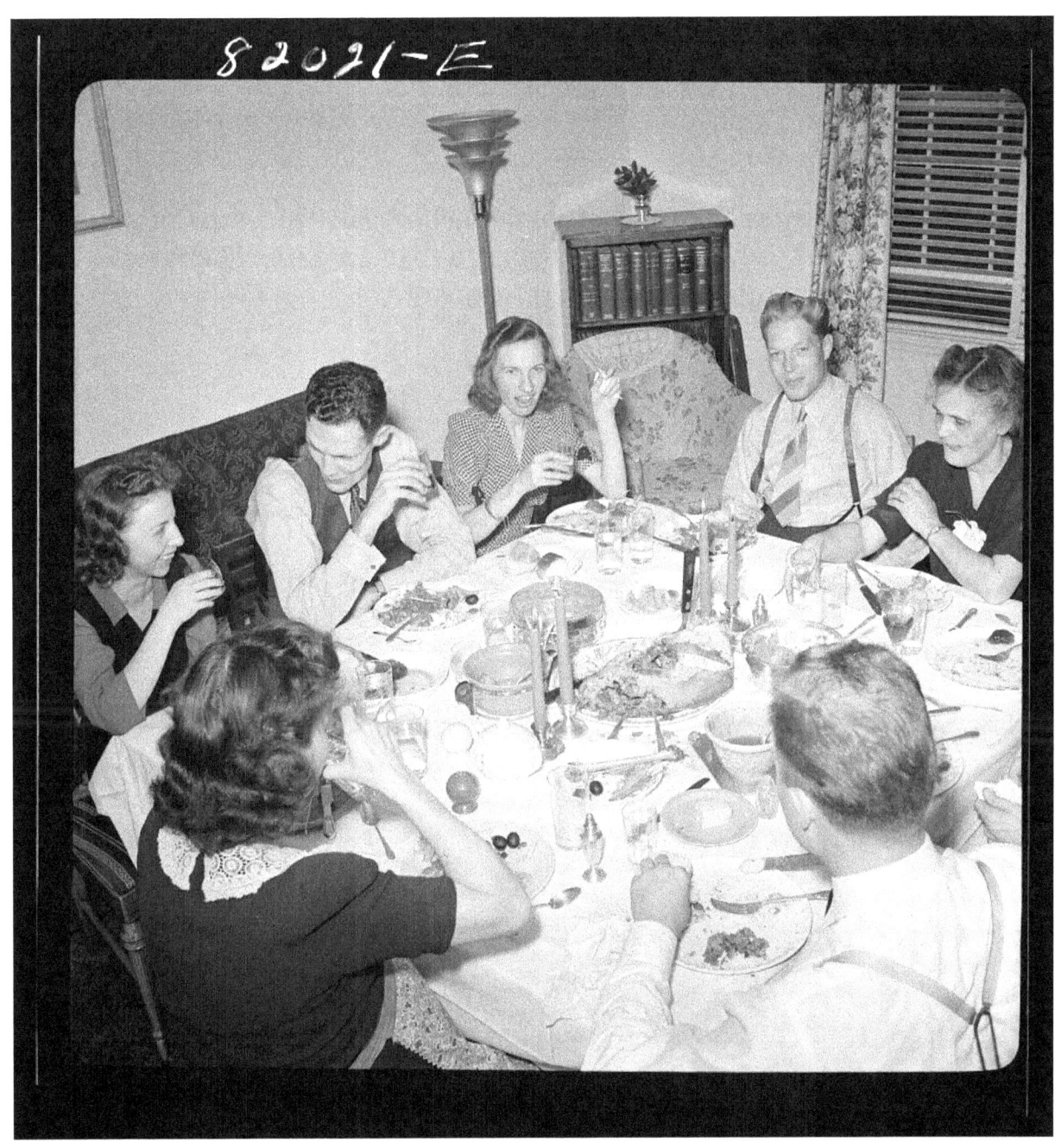

"Red Cross nurse alongside of soldier in hospital bed, with Christmas decorations." Created between 1915 and 1930. Library of Congress. http://www.loc.gov/pictures/item/93505085/

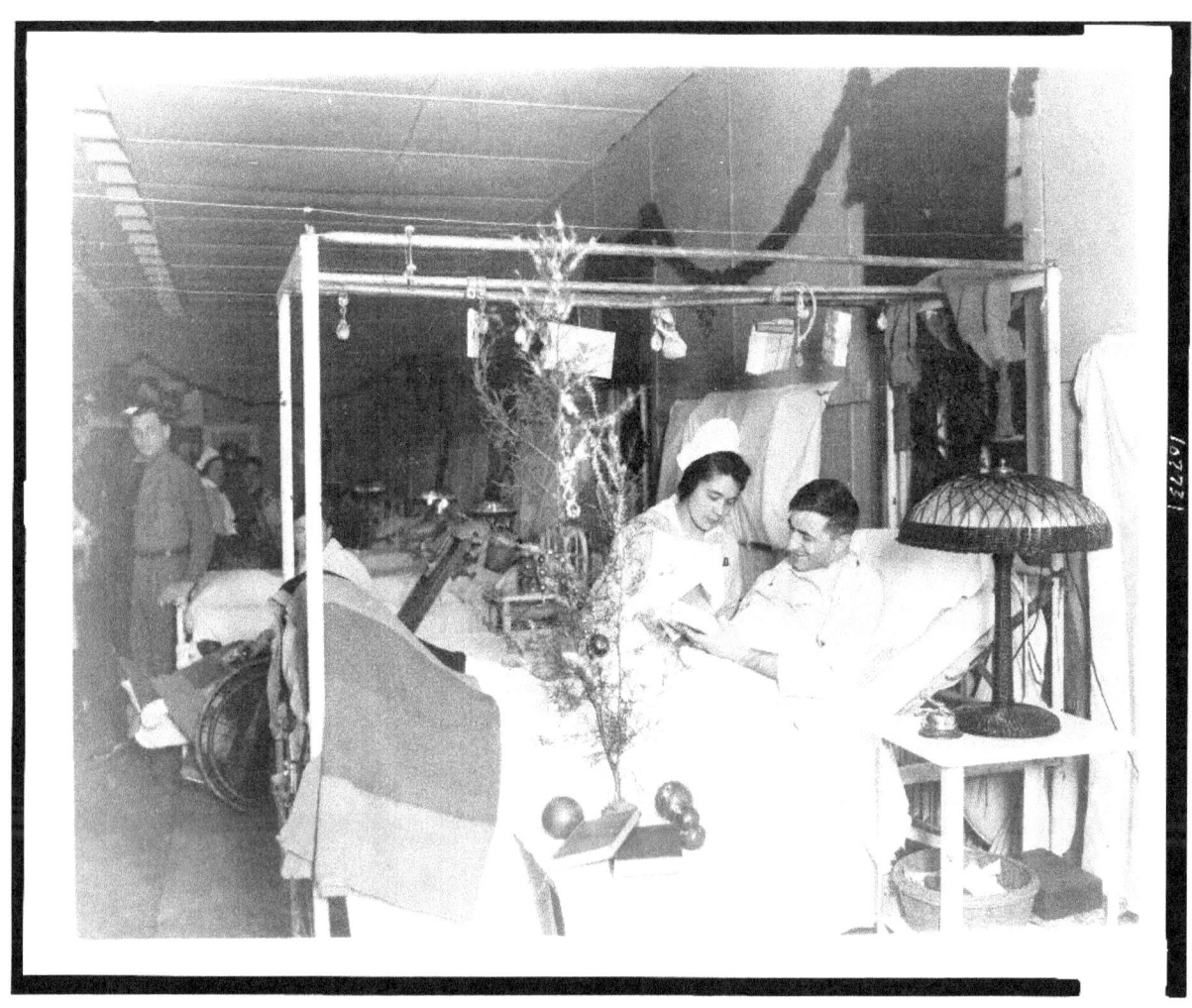

"Christmas Tree at the District Jail, Washington, D.C., and some of the Prisoners." Created between 1909 and 1932. Library of Congress. http://www.loc.gov/pictures/item/96507322/

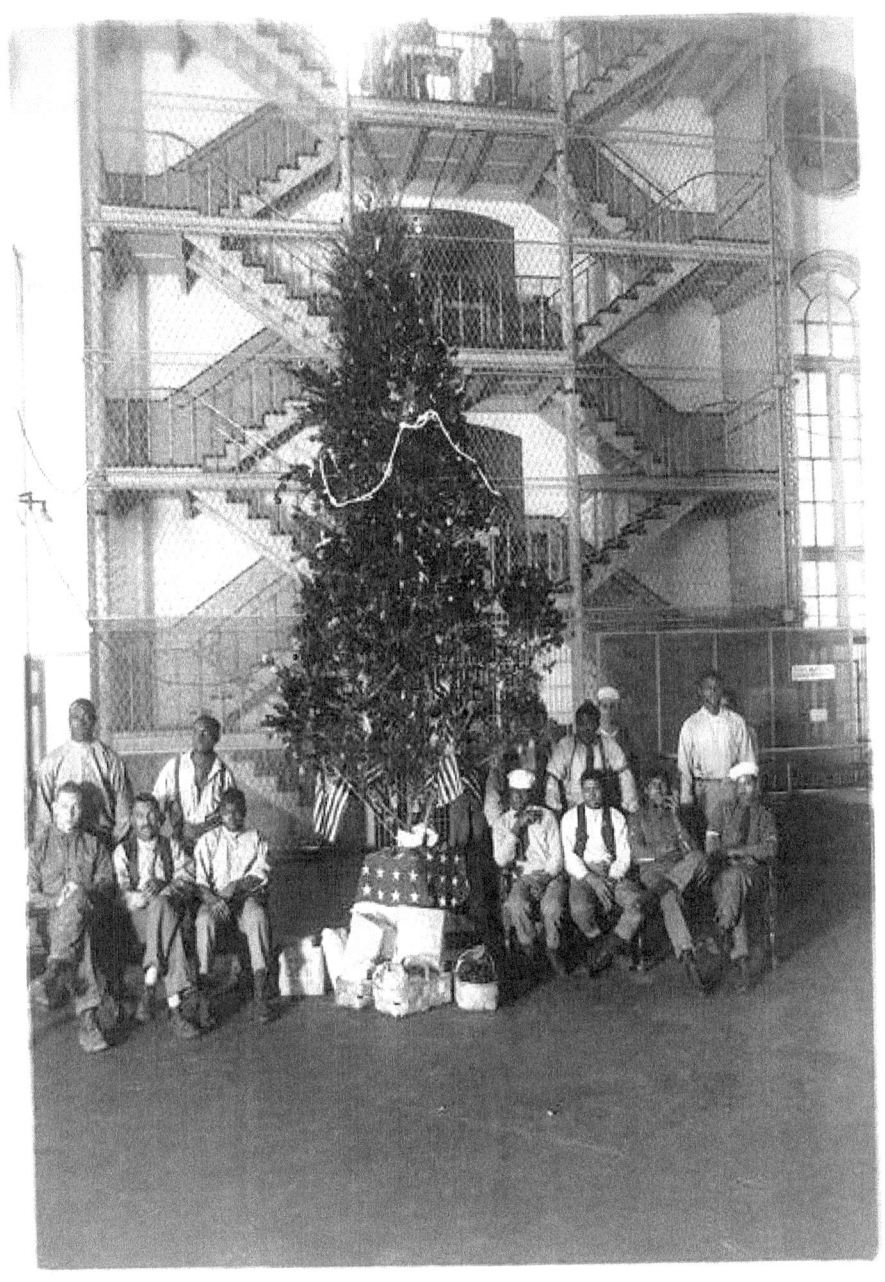

"Boy Beside Store Window Display of Christmas Ornaments." Created between 1941 and 1942. Library of Congress.
http://www.loc.gov/pictures/item/2017877958/

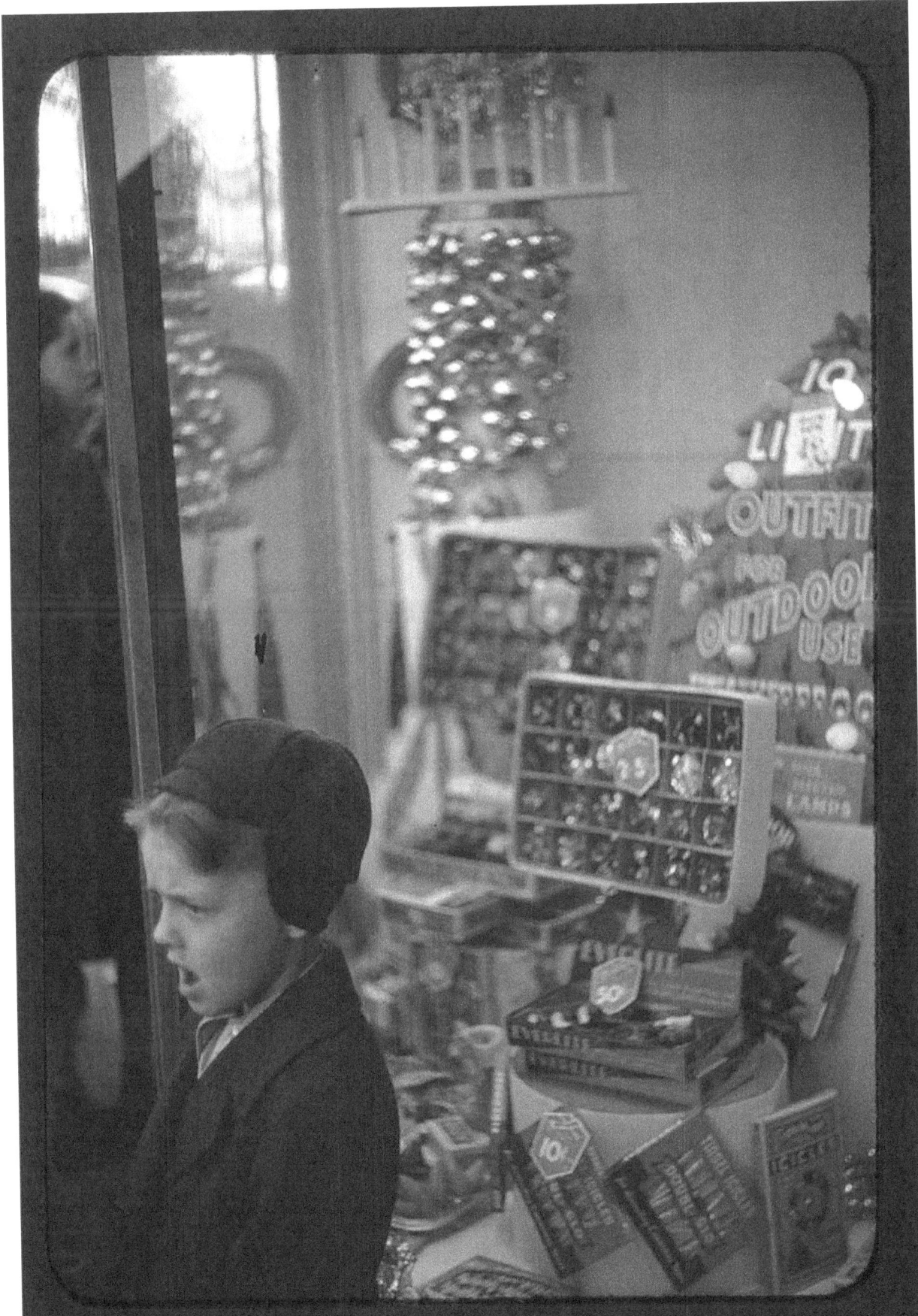

Detroit Publishing Company. "Remember the Poor: A Salvation Army Christmas Box." c. 1903. Library of Congress: http://www.loc.gov/pictures/item/2016798929/

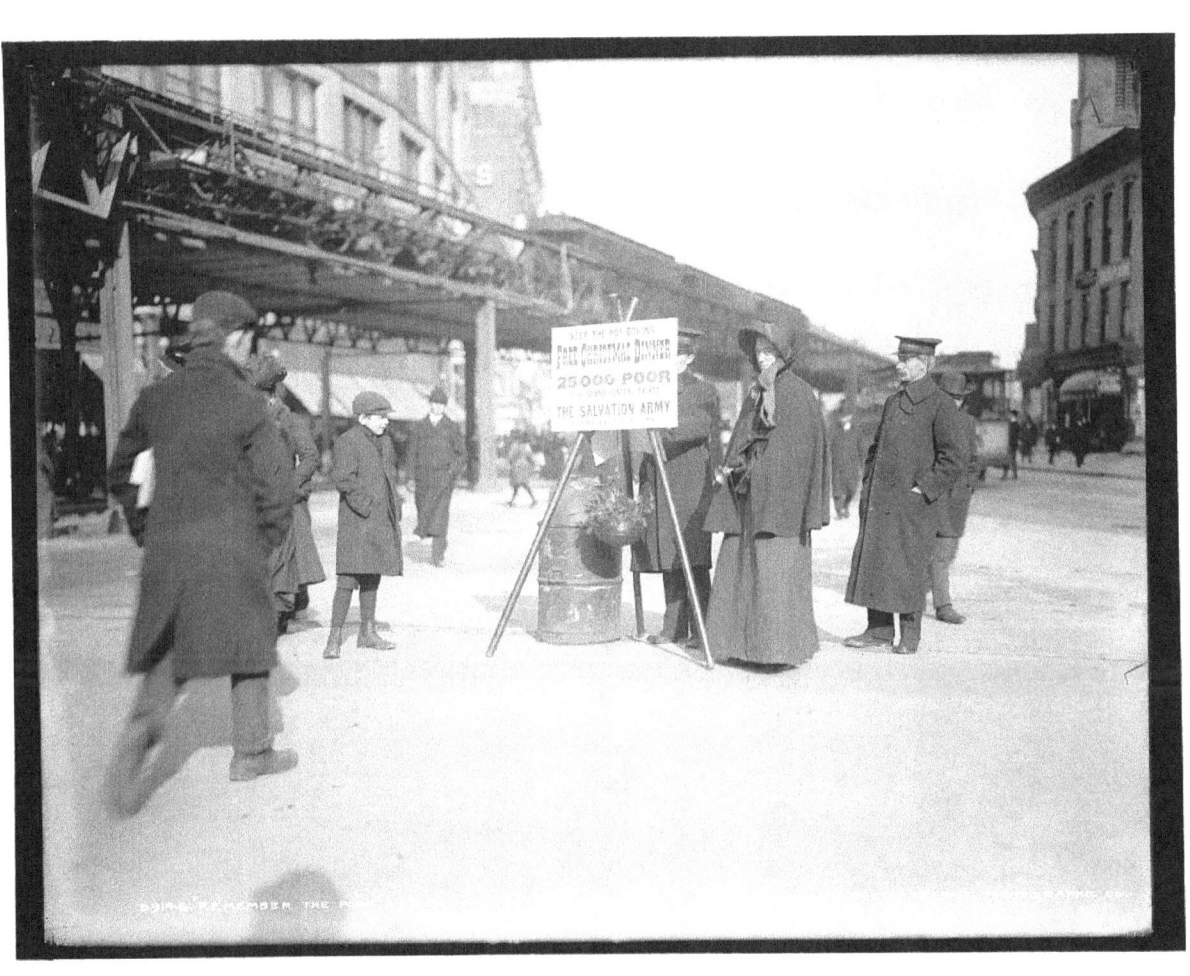

Collier, John, Jr. "Christmas in the Home of a Government Executive in Virginia." Falls Church, Va. Christmas Day, 1941. Library of Congress. http://www.loc.gov/pictures/item/2017821835/

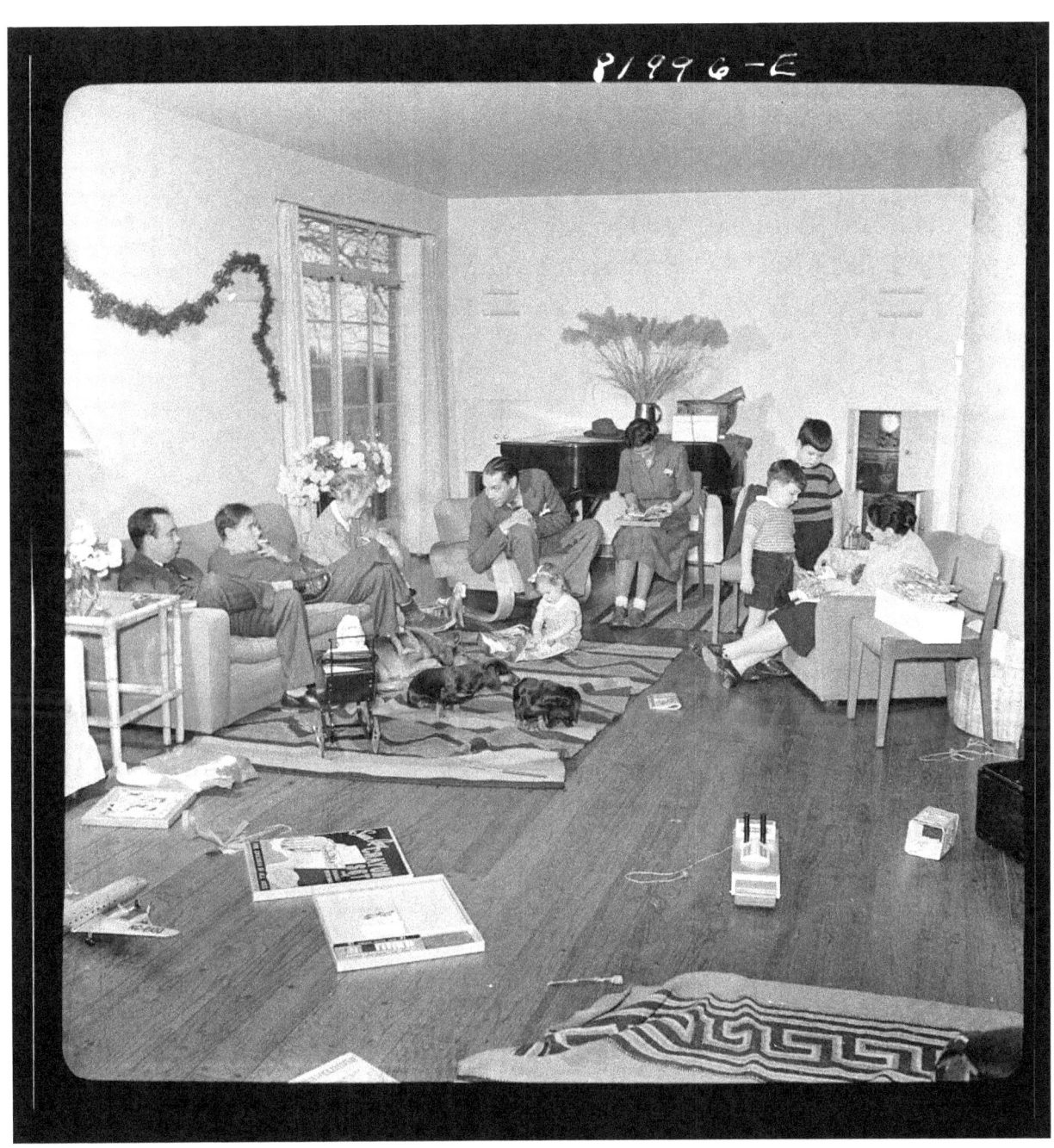

Collier, John, Jr. "Christmas in the Home of a Government Executive, Virginia." December 1941. Library of Congress. http://www.loc.gov/pictures/item/2017821856/

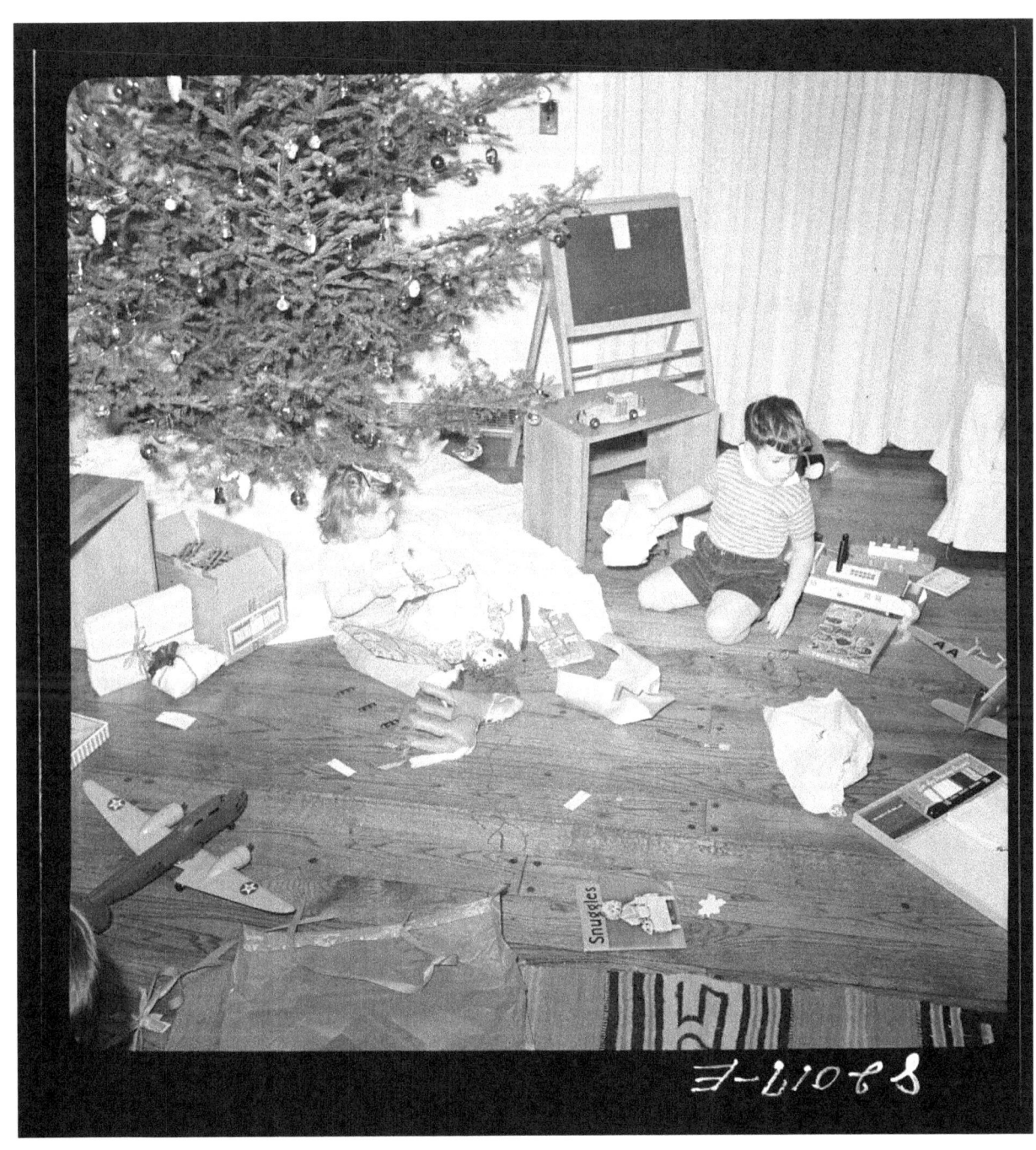

"Christmas Morning." c. 1909. Library of Congress.
http://www.loc.gov/pictures/item/2005693074/

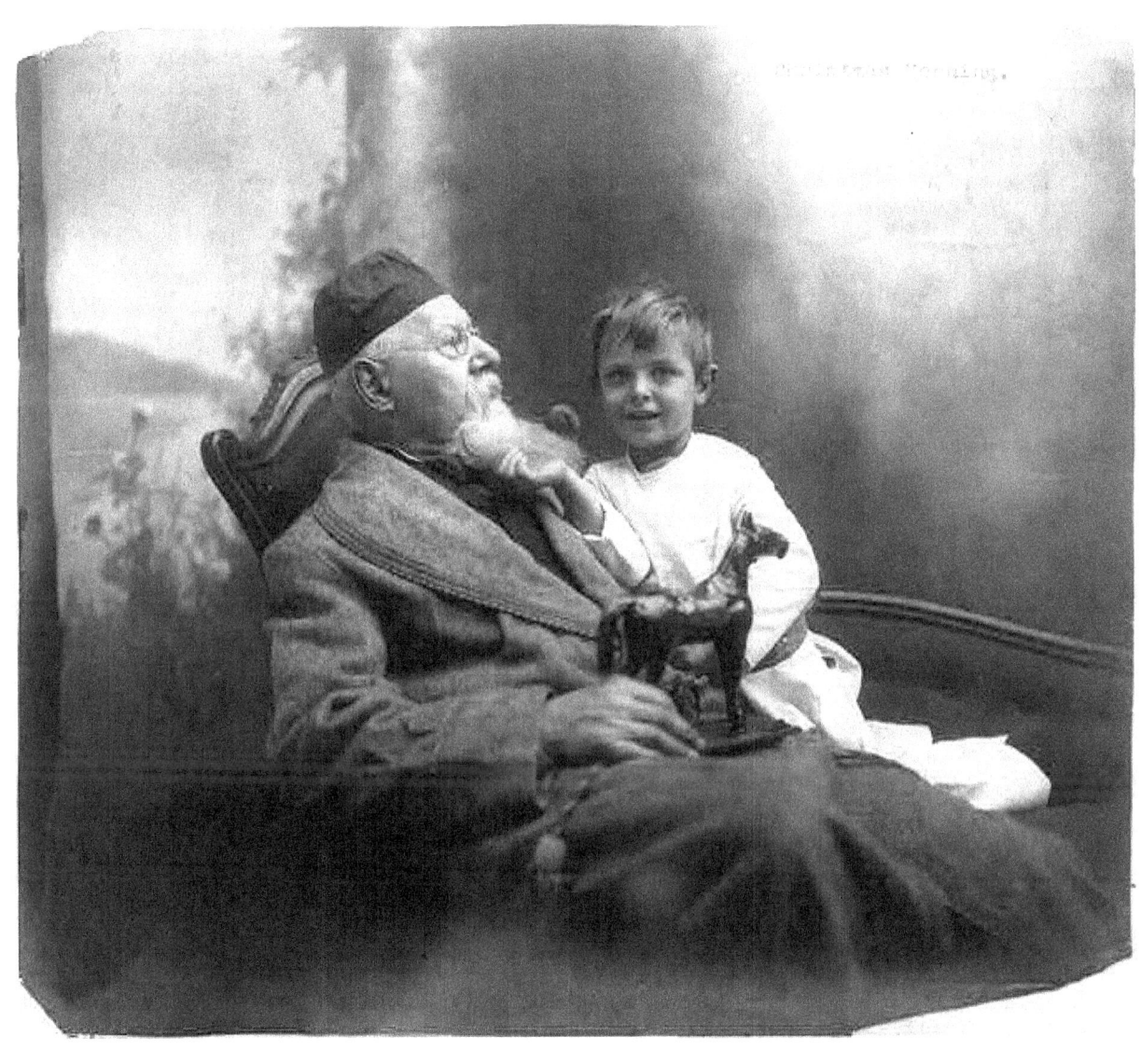

Delano, Jack. "Snow in Providence, Rhode Island." December 1940. Library of Congress. http://www.loc.gov/pictures/item/2017748741/

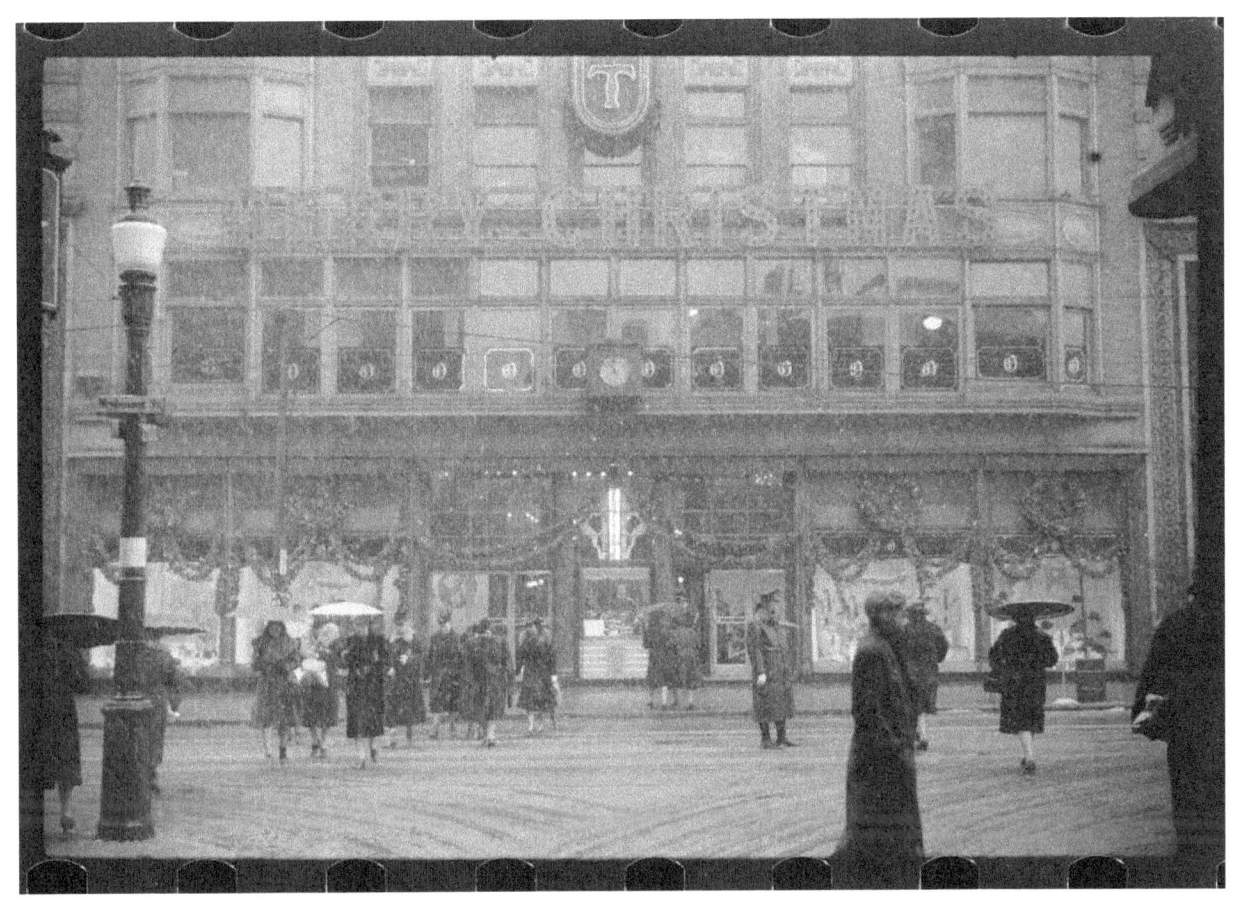

Delano, Jack. "Christmas Window Display in a 5 and 10, Providence, Rhode Island. December 1940. Library of Congress. http://www.loc.gov/pictures/item/2017748757/

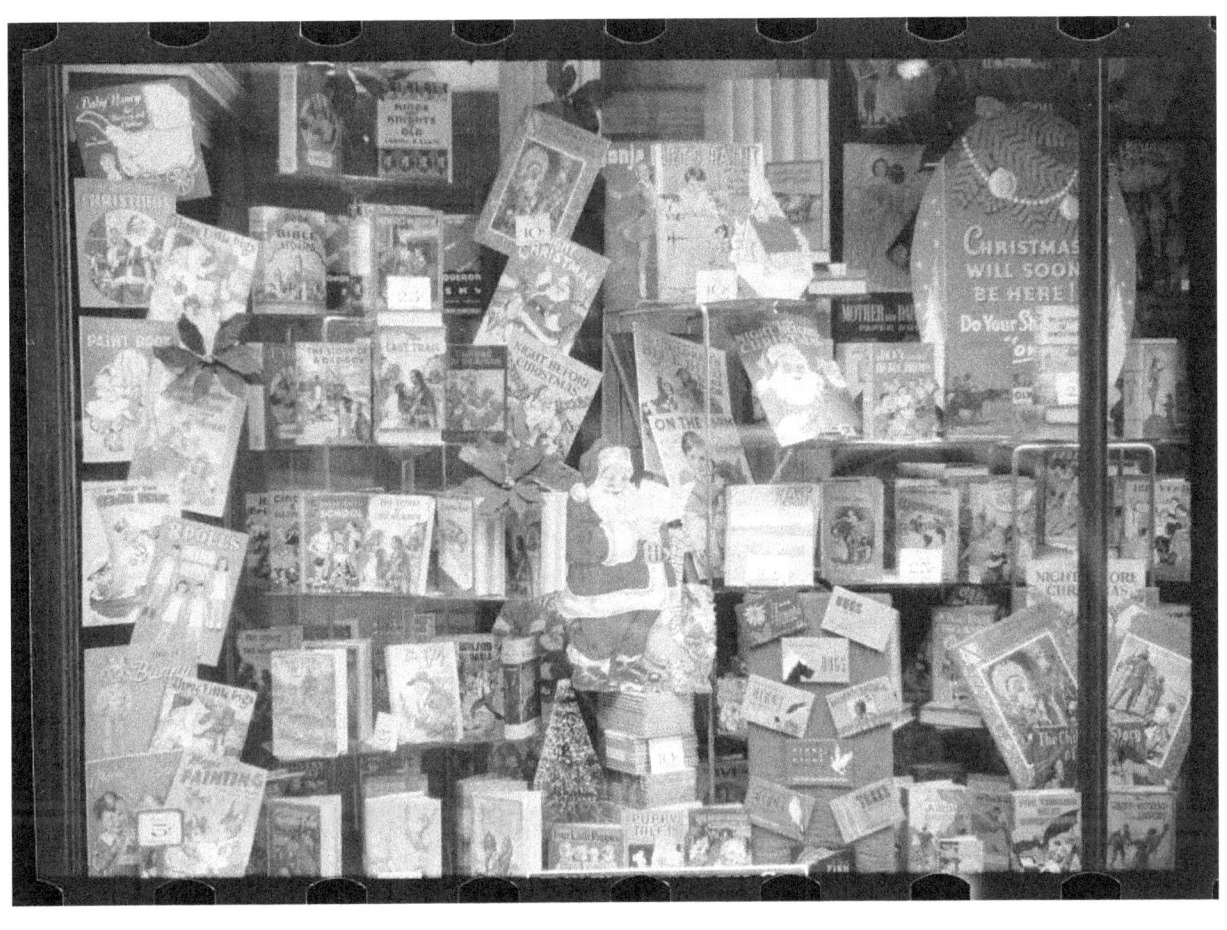

Delano, Jack. "Window Shoppers Watching Toy Display in Downtown Providence, Rhode Island." December 1940. Library of Congress. http://www.loc.gov/pictures/item/2017748764/

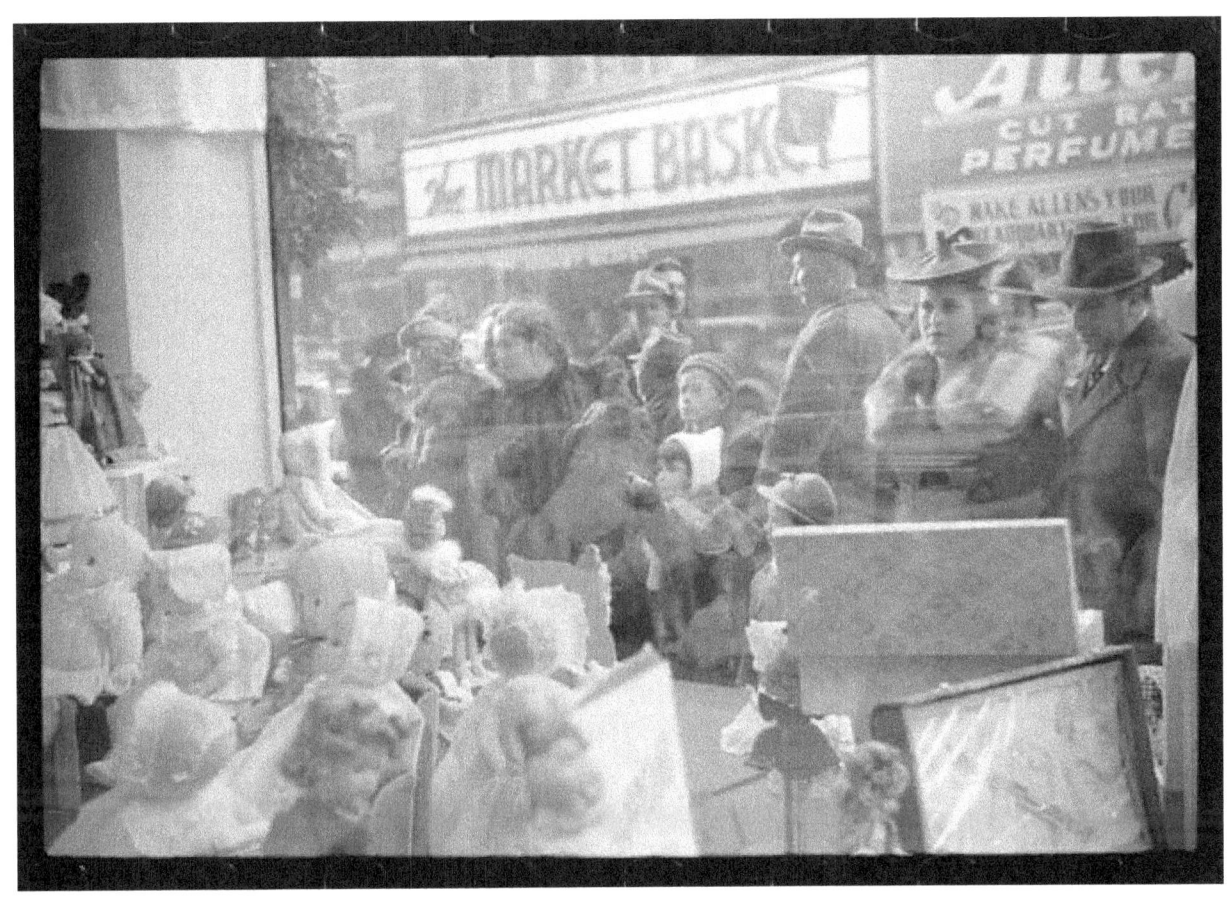

Delano, Jack. "Window Shoppers Watching Toy Display in Downtown Providence, Rhode Island." December 1940. Library of Congress.

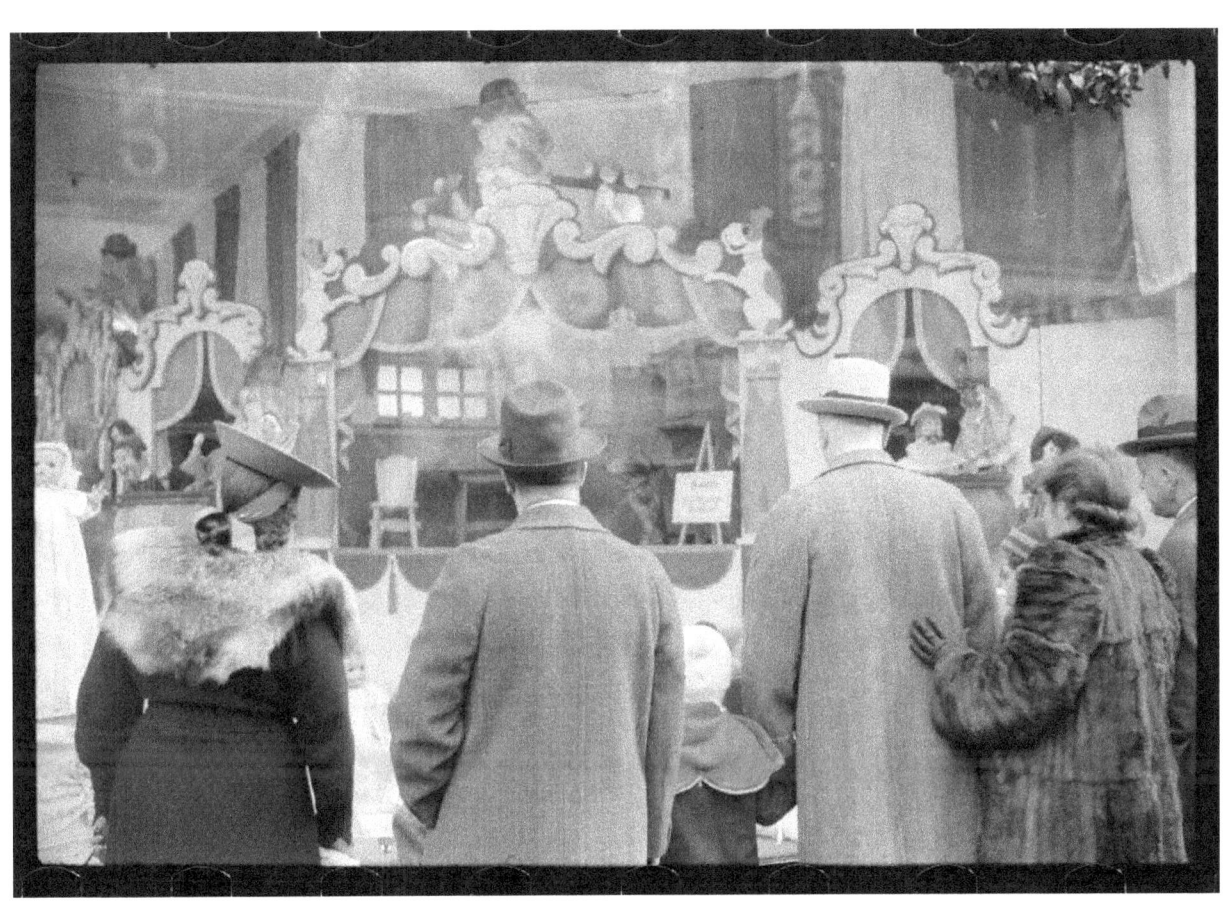

"African Americans selling Christmas Trees and Holly, Washington, D.C." ca. 1920. Library of Congress.
http://www.loc.gov/pictures/item/2001706171/

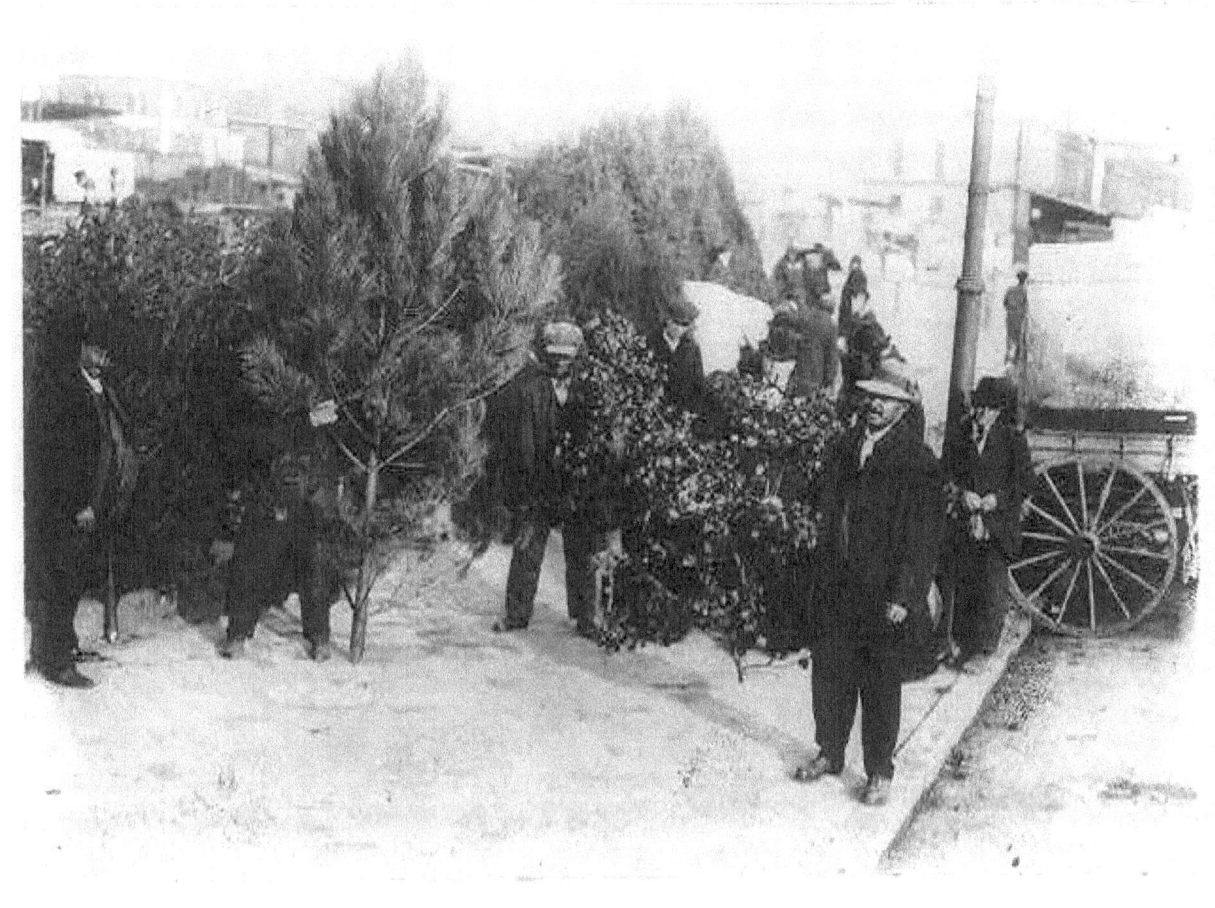

"Christmas Window Display at an Unidentified Oldsmobile Dealers, Probably in Washington, D. C." 1921? Library of Congress. http://www.loc.gov/pictures/item/2001706319/

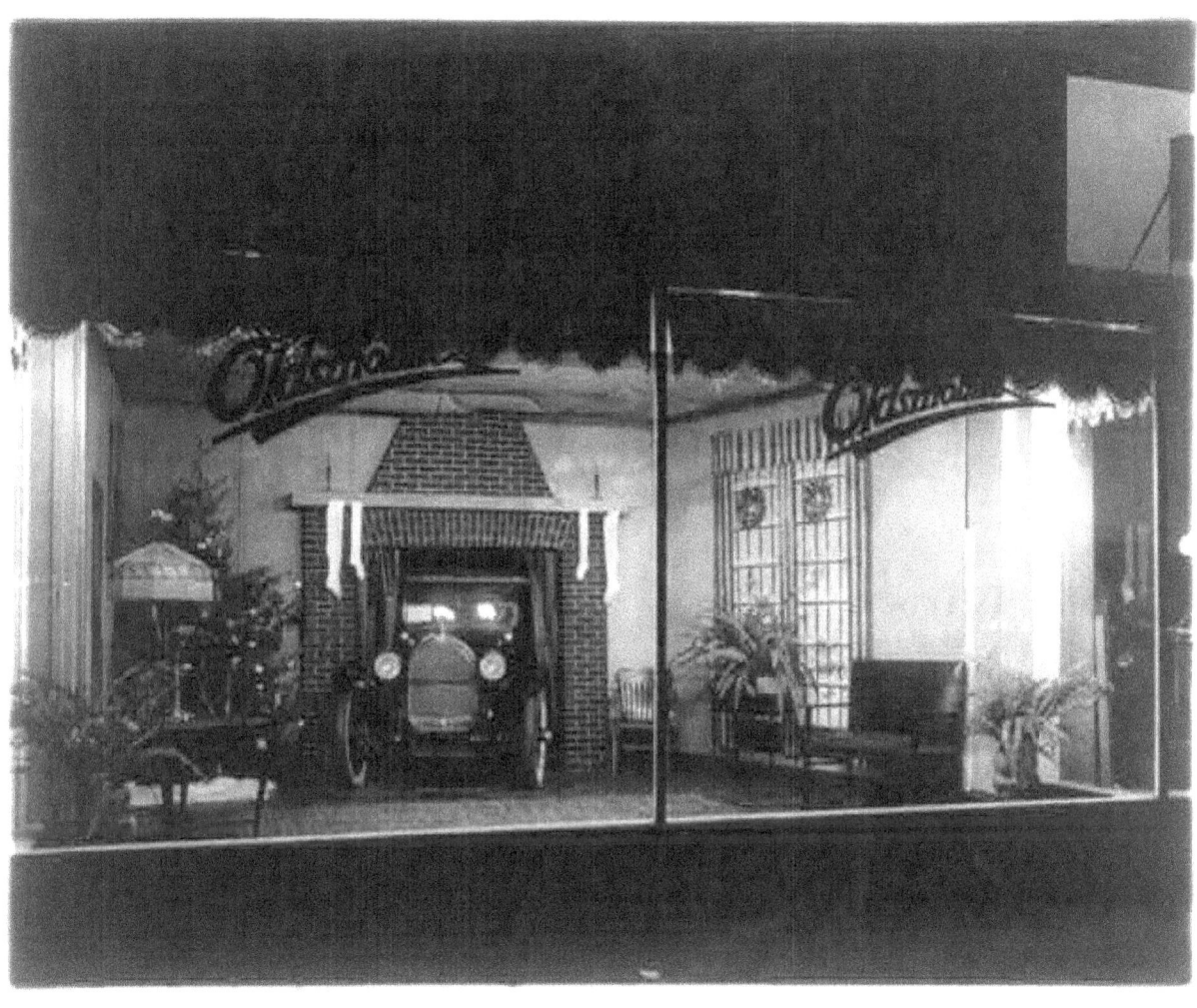

"American Soldiers Opening Red Cross Christmas Boxes." February 18, 1918. Library of Congress.
http://www.loc.gov/pictures/item/2017672382/

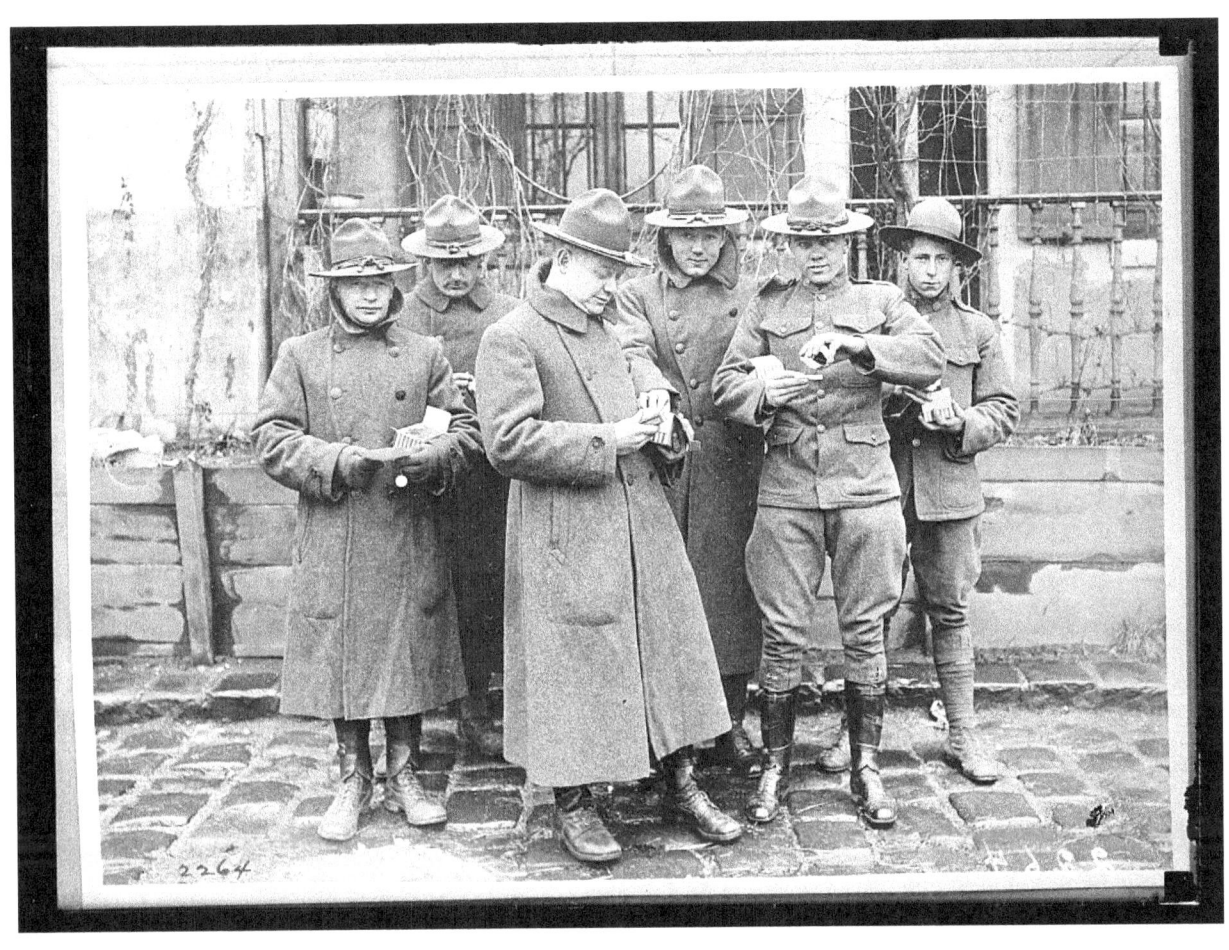

Gottscho-Schleisner, Inc. "Rockefeller Center. Plaza Christmas Decorations." December 9, 1943. Library of Congress.

http://www.loc.gov/pictures/item/gsc1994000426/PP/

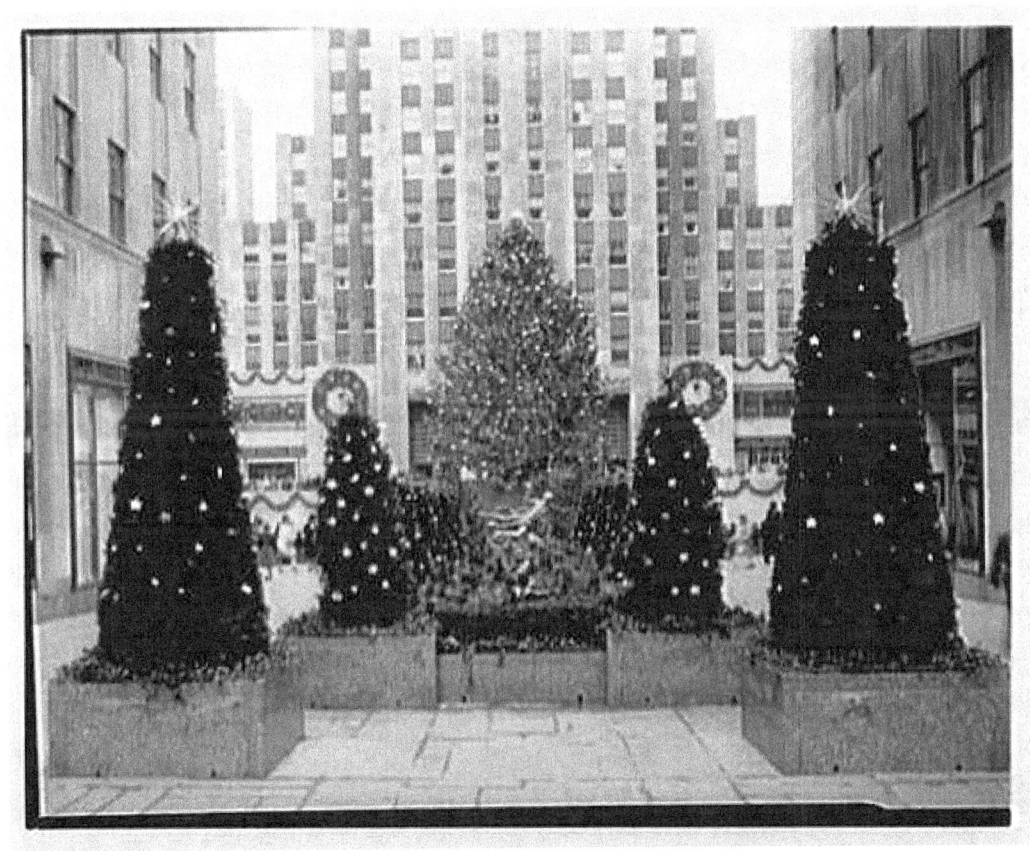

American Colony (Jerusalem). "During Christmas Services in Church of Nativity, Bethlehem." Between 1934 and 1939. Library of Congress. http://www.loc.gov/pictures/item/mpc2004000093/PP/

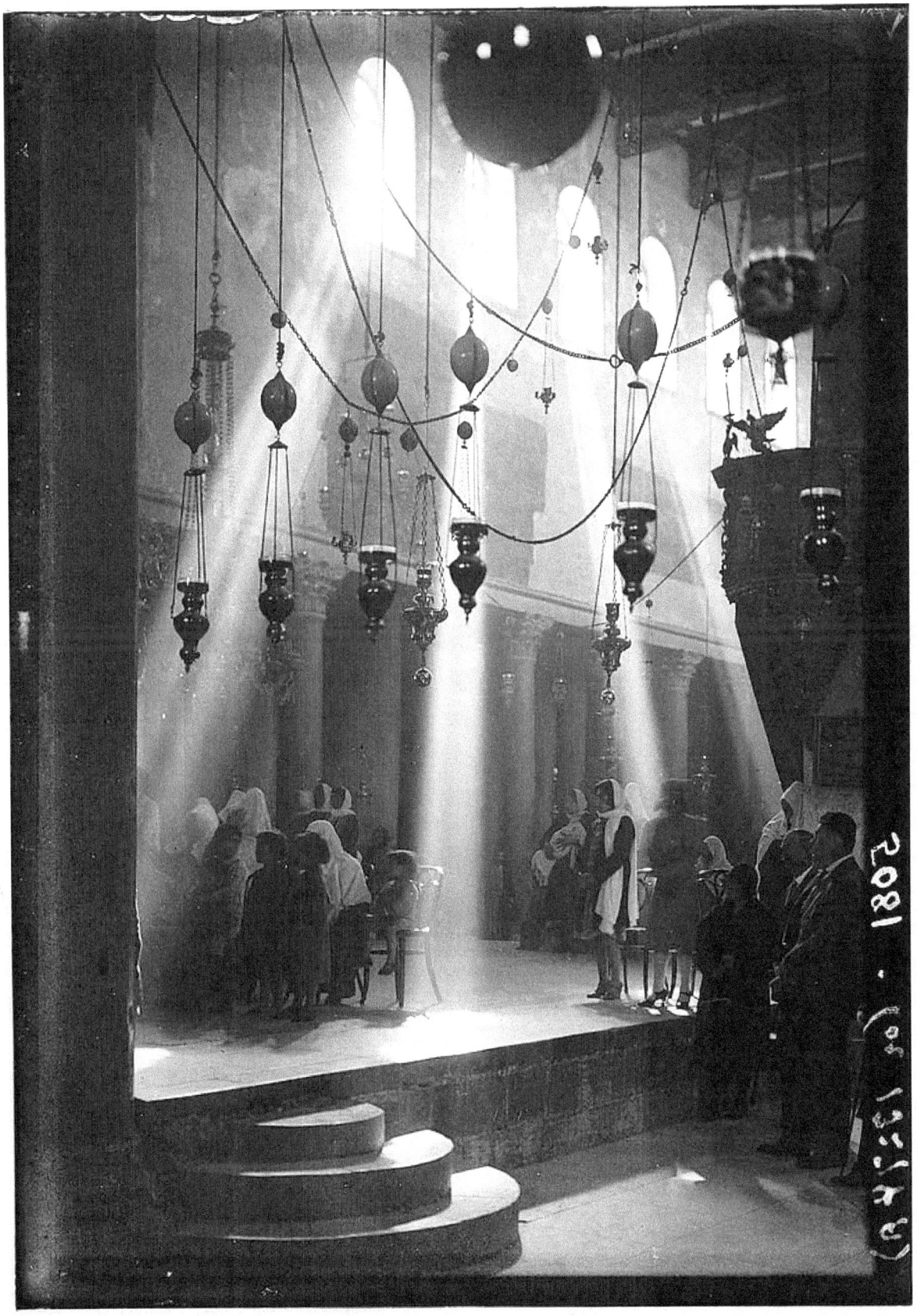

"Christmas in Bethlehem, Religious Procession." Between 1898 and 1946. Library of Congress.
http://www.loc.gov/pictures/item/mpc2005001315/PP/

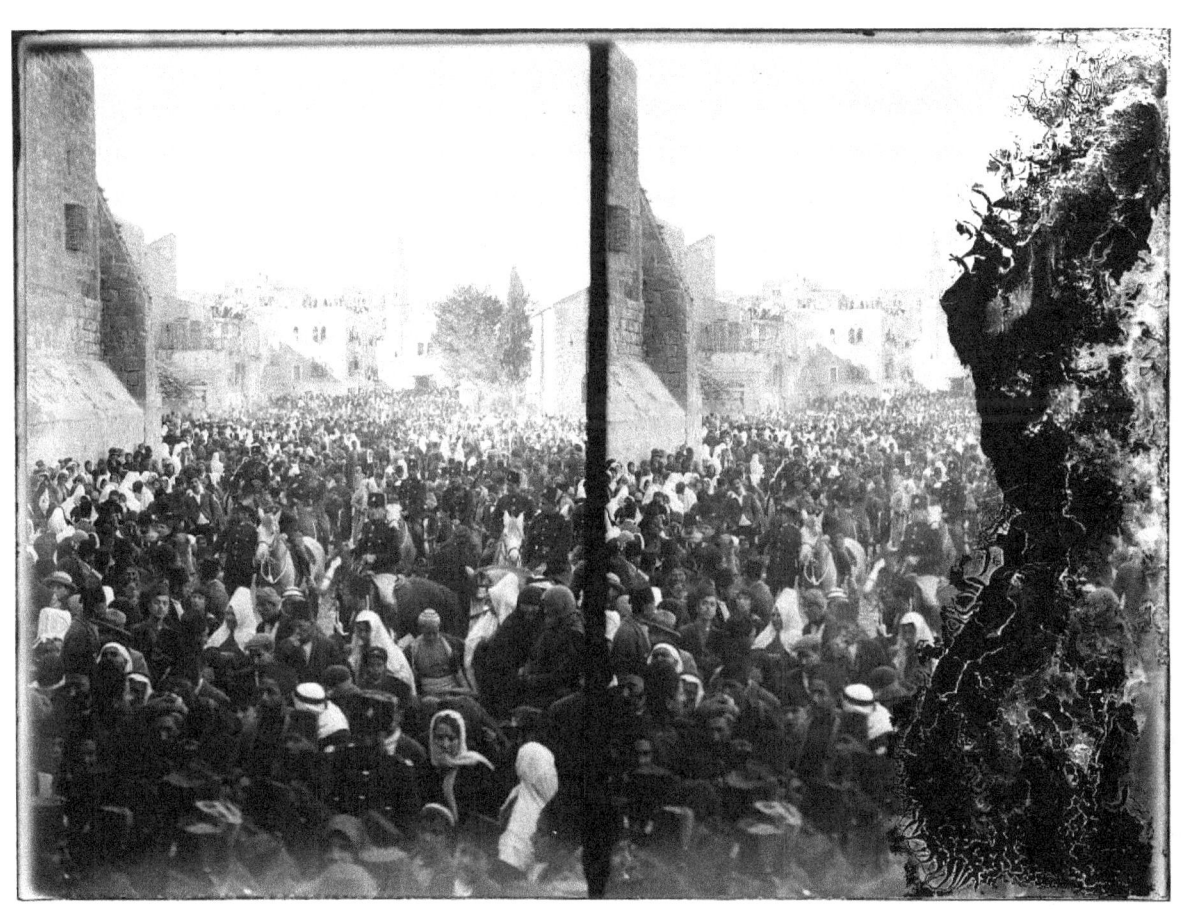

Matson Photo Service. "Australian Soldiers at Xmas." Between 1940 and 1946. http://www.loc.gov/pictures/item/mpc2005009756/PP/

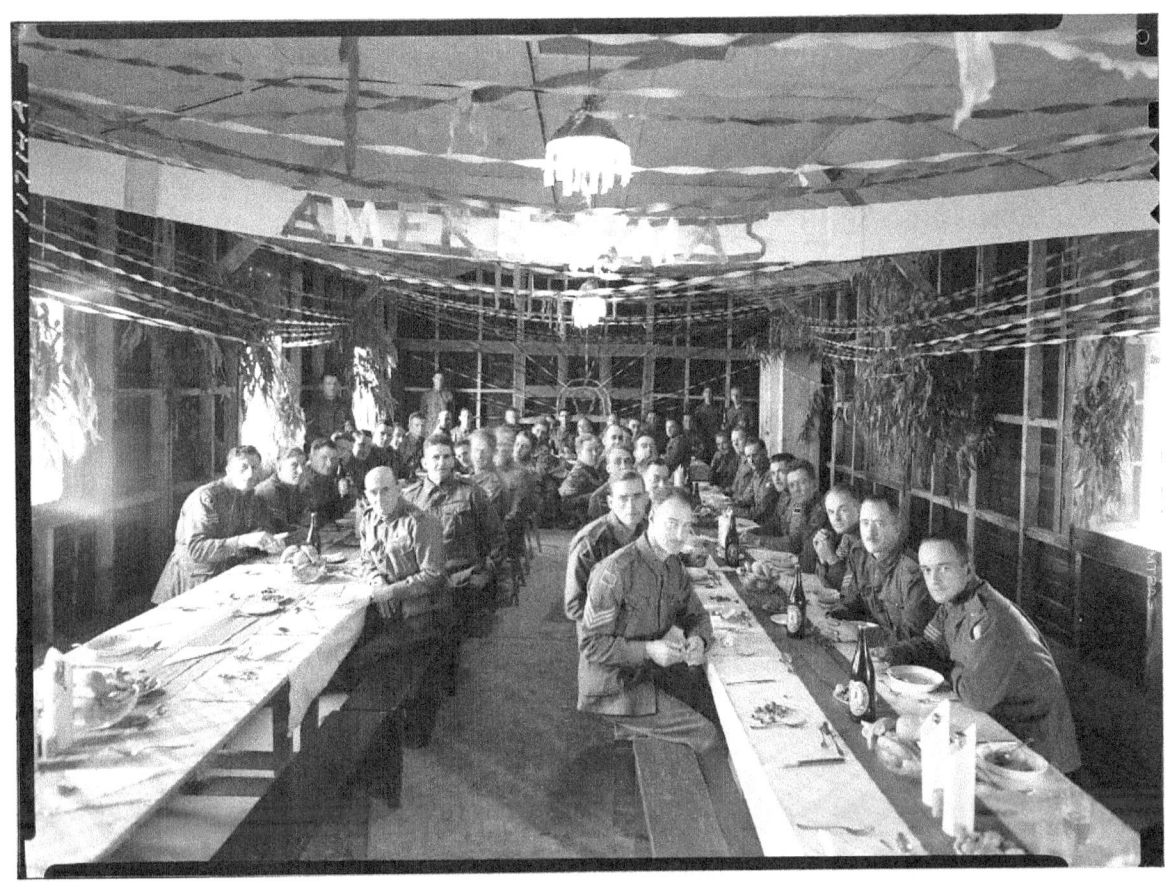

Matson Photo Service. "Military Y.M.C.A. Xmas Festivities, Australian." Between 1940 and 1946.

http://www.loc.gov/pictures/item/mpc2005010057/PP/

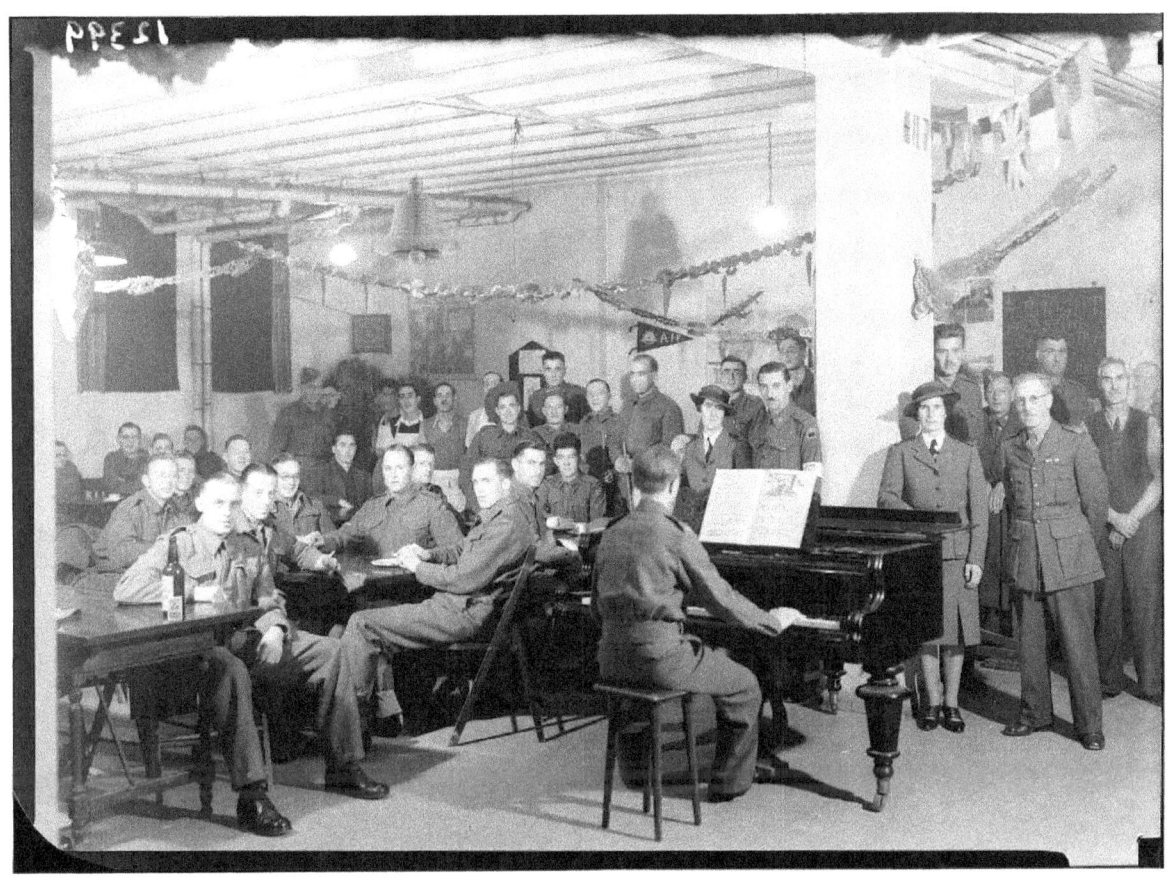

Underwood & Underwood. "Emigrants in 'Pens' at Ellis Island, New York, Probably on or Near Christmas." C. 1906. Library of Congress. http://www.loc.gov/pictures/item/2012646352/

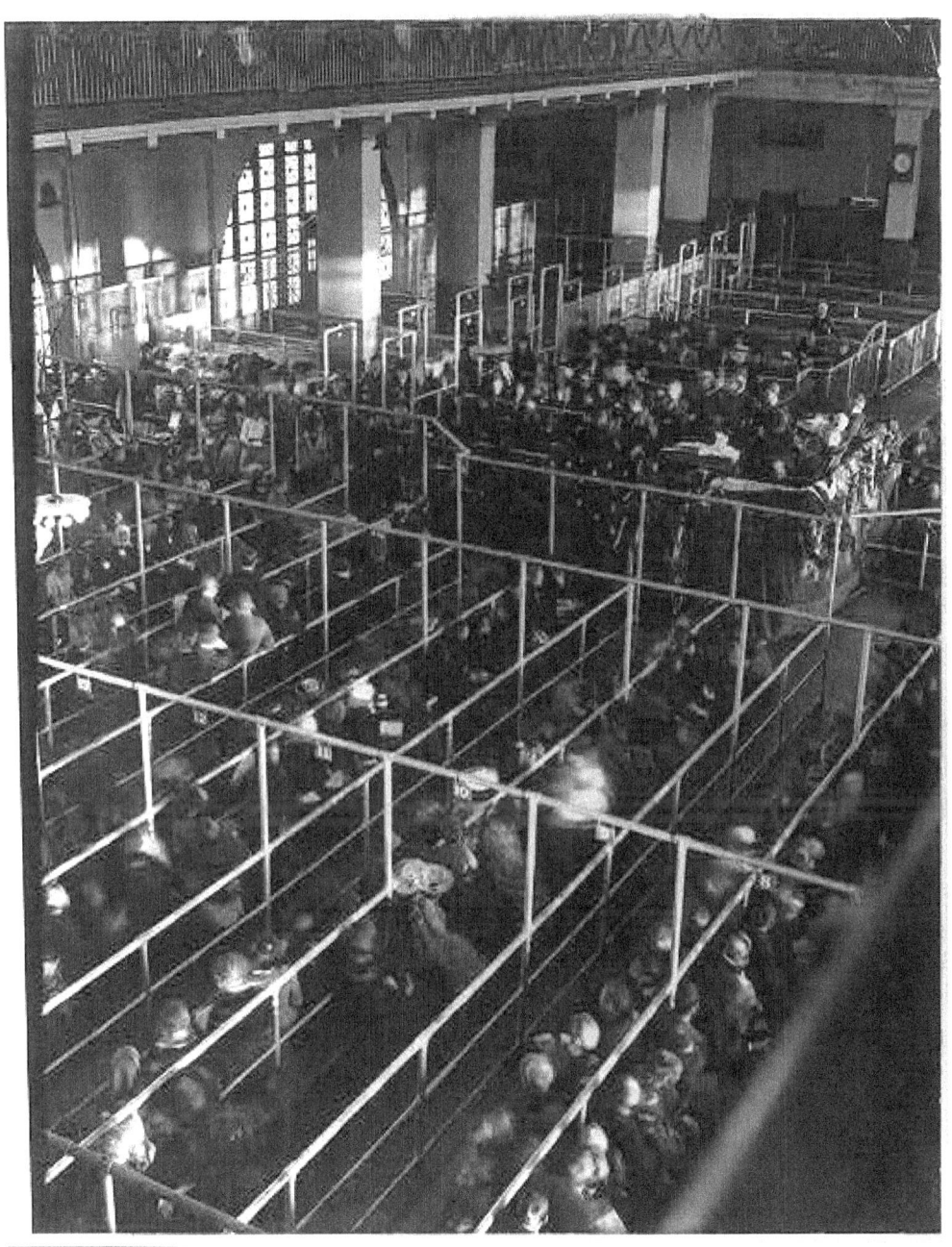

"Orphan Children, Syrians, Armenians, Jews and other nationalities cared for by S. AND P. Relief fund in the Austrian Hospice building, Jerusalem."
October 28, 1918. Library of Congress.
http://www.loc.gov/pictures/item/2017668101/

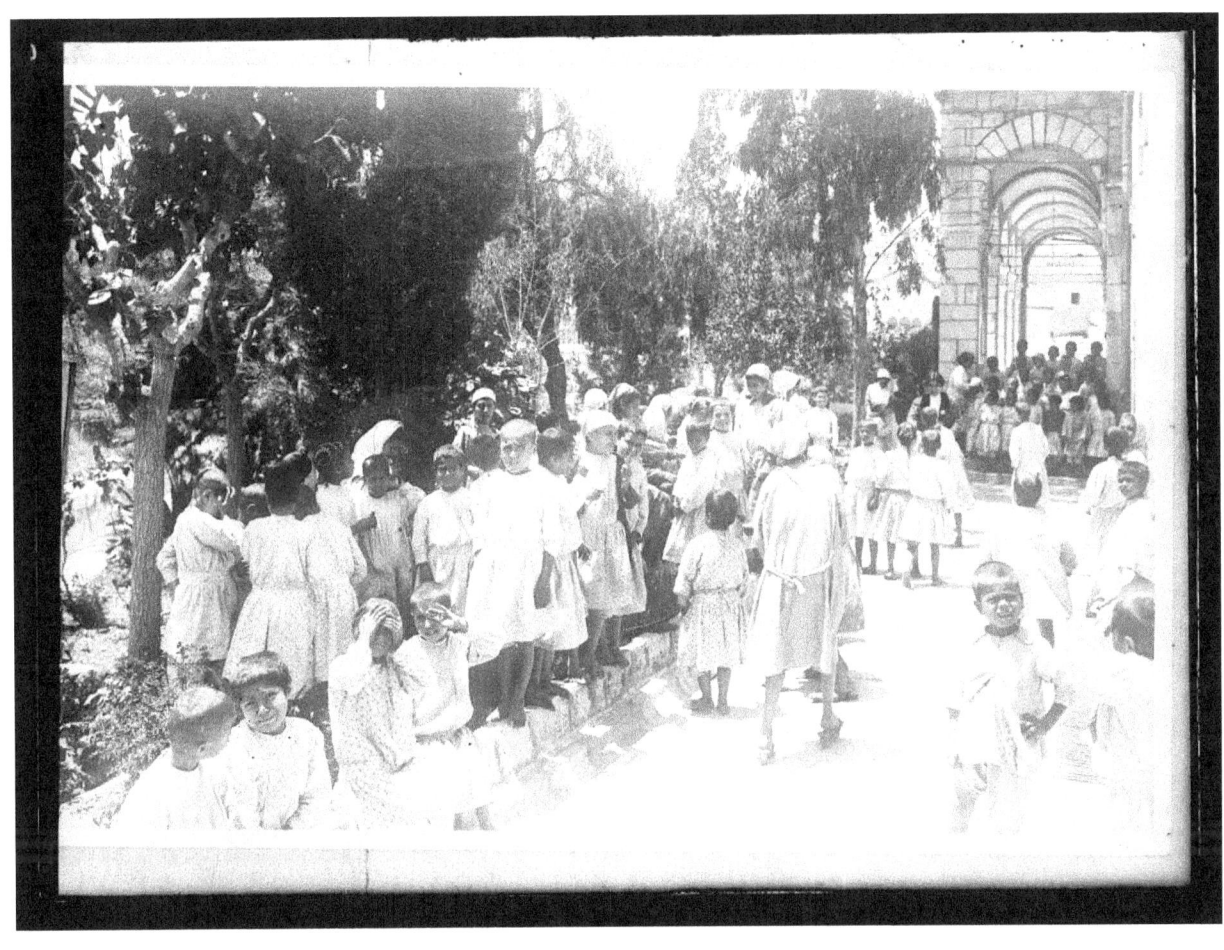

"Christmas Kits Ready to be Shipped to France for Distribution among the American Soldiers Fighting in the Trenches." Between 1917 and 1920. Library of Congress.
http://www.loc.gov/pictures/item/2017672184/

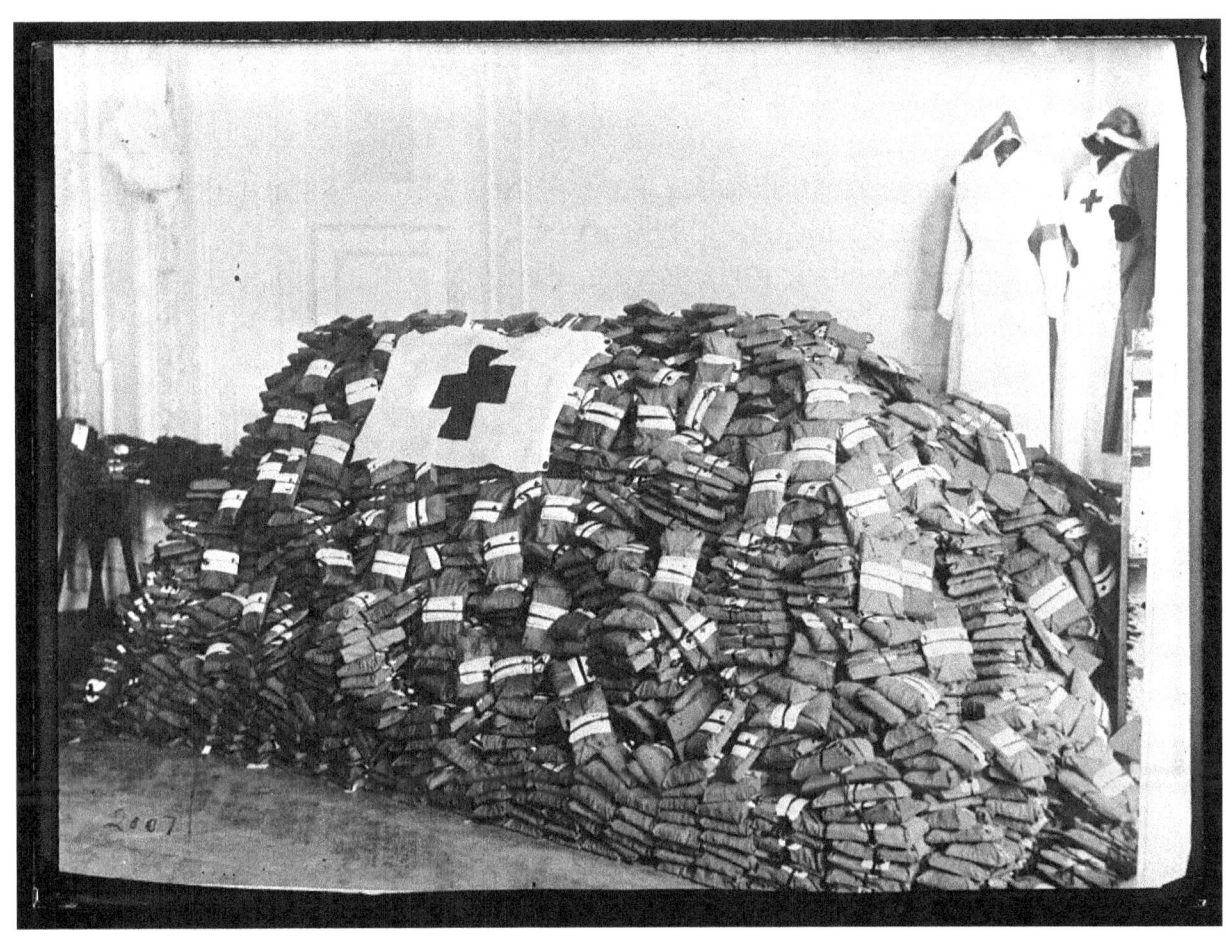

"Room with Christmas Tree--Harold Lloyd Estate, Beverly Hills, Los Angeles County, CA." Library of Congress. http://www.loc.gov/pictures/item/ca0198.photos.011637p/

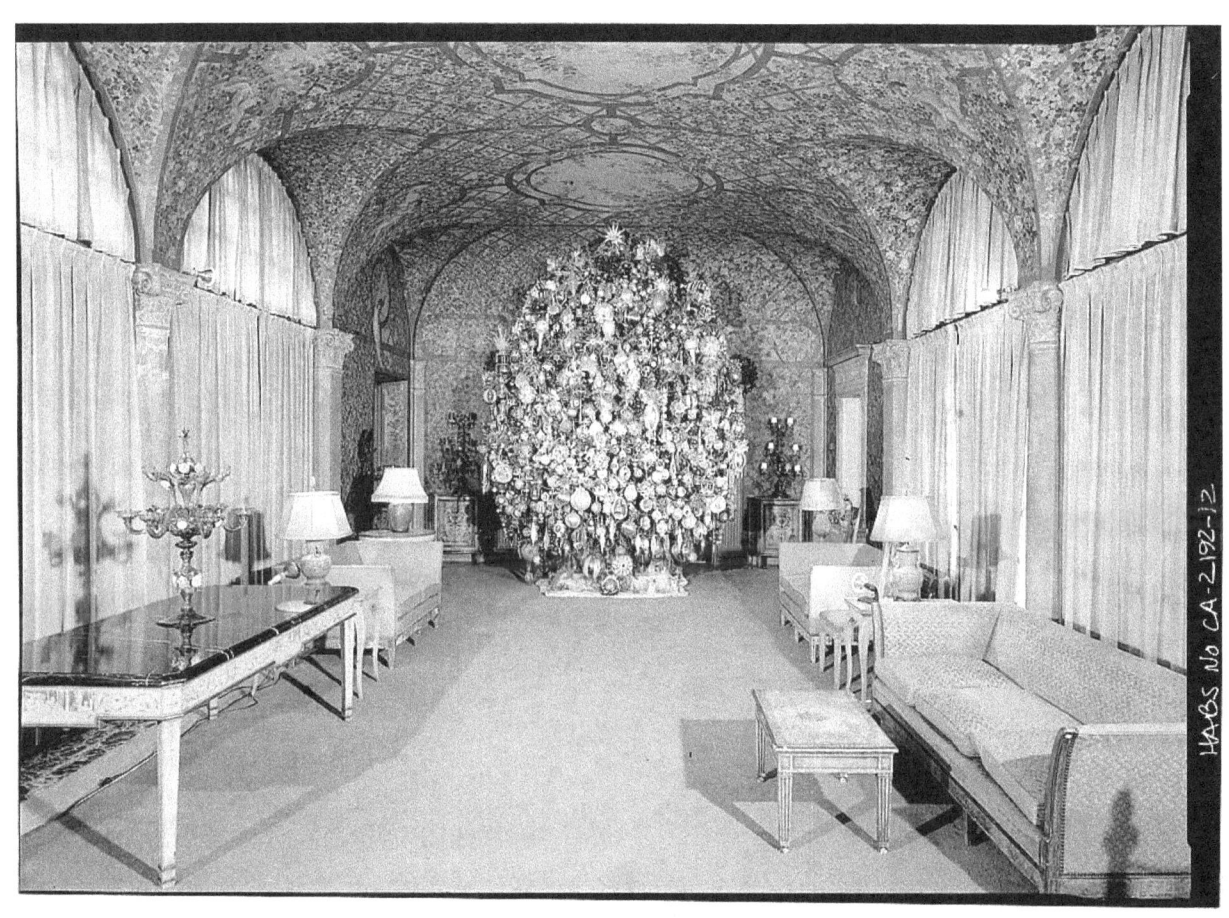

Christmas Tree in Rotunda--City of Paris Dry Goods Company, Geary & Stockton Streets, San Francisco, San Francisco County, CA. Library of Congress. http://www.loc.gov/pictures/item/ca0632.photos.016207p/

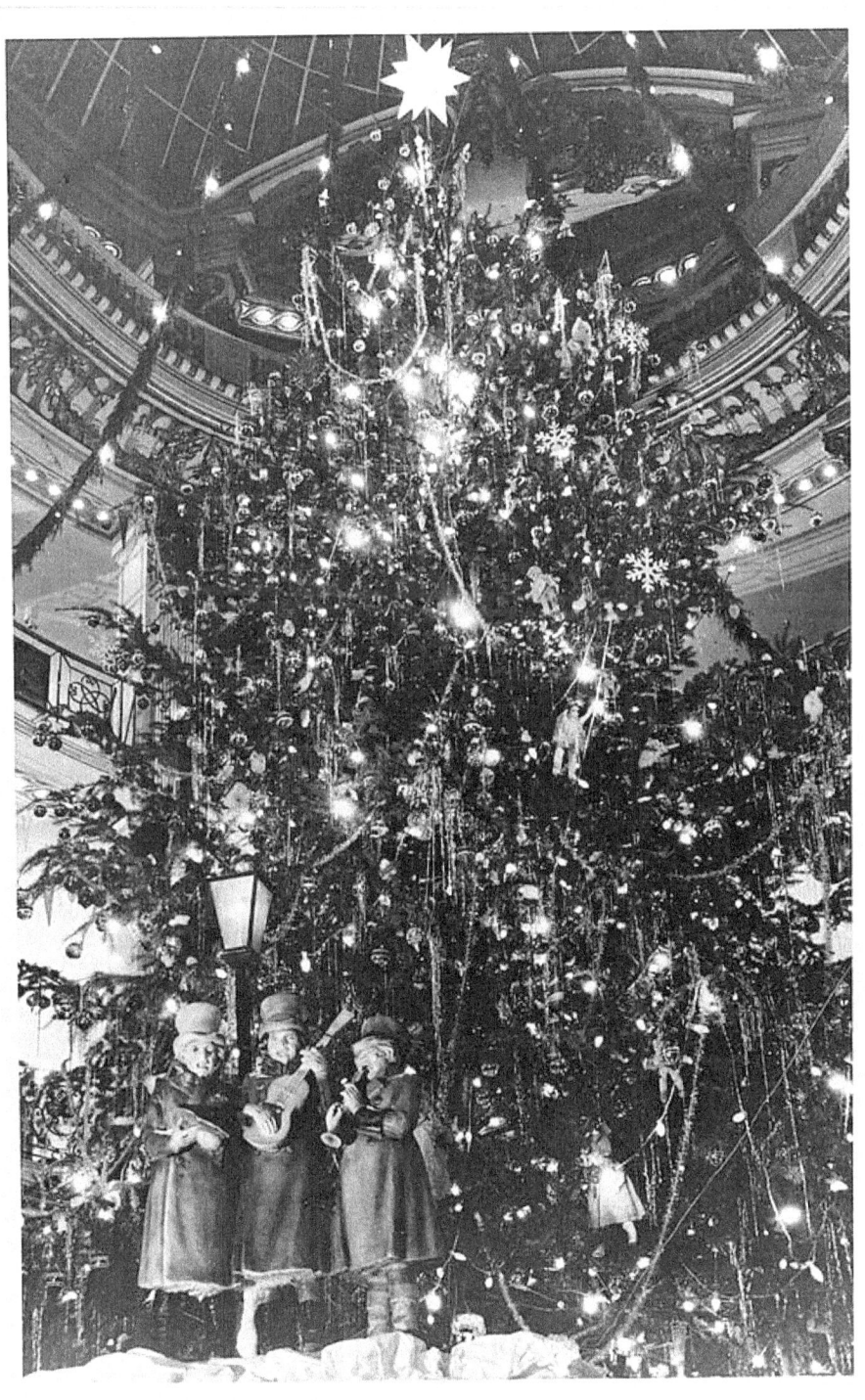

Delano, Jack. "Hanging Christmas Decorations in Providence, Rhode Island." December 1940.
http://www.loc.gov/pictures/item/2017748683/

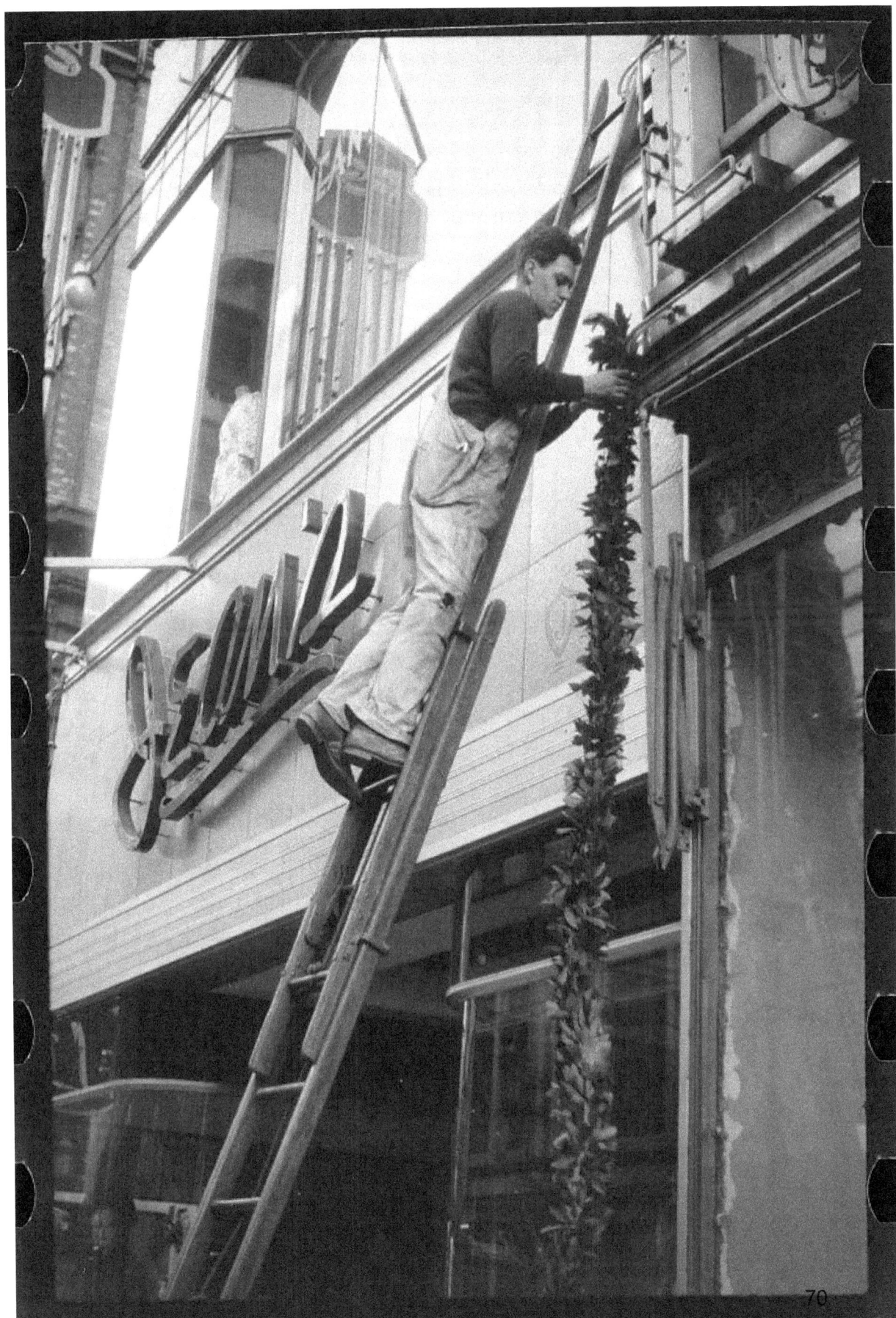

Delano, Jack. "Little Girl Playing with her Christmas Presents on a Side Street in Charlotte Amalie, Virgin Islands." December 1941. http://www.loc.gov/pictures/item/2017751430/

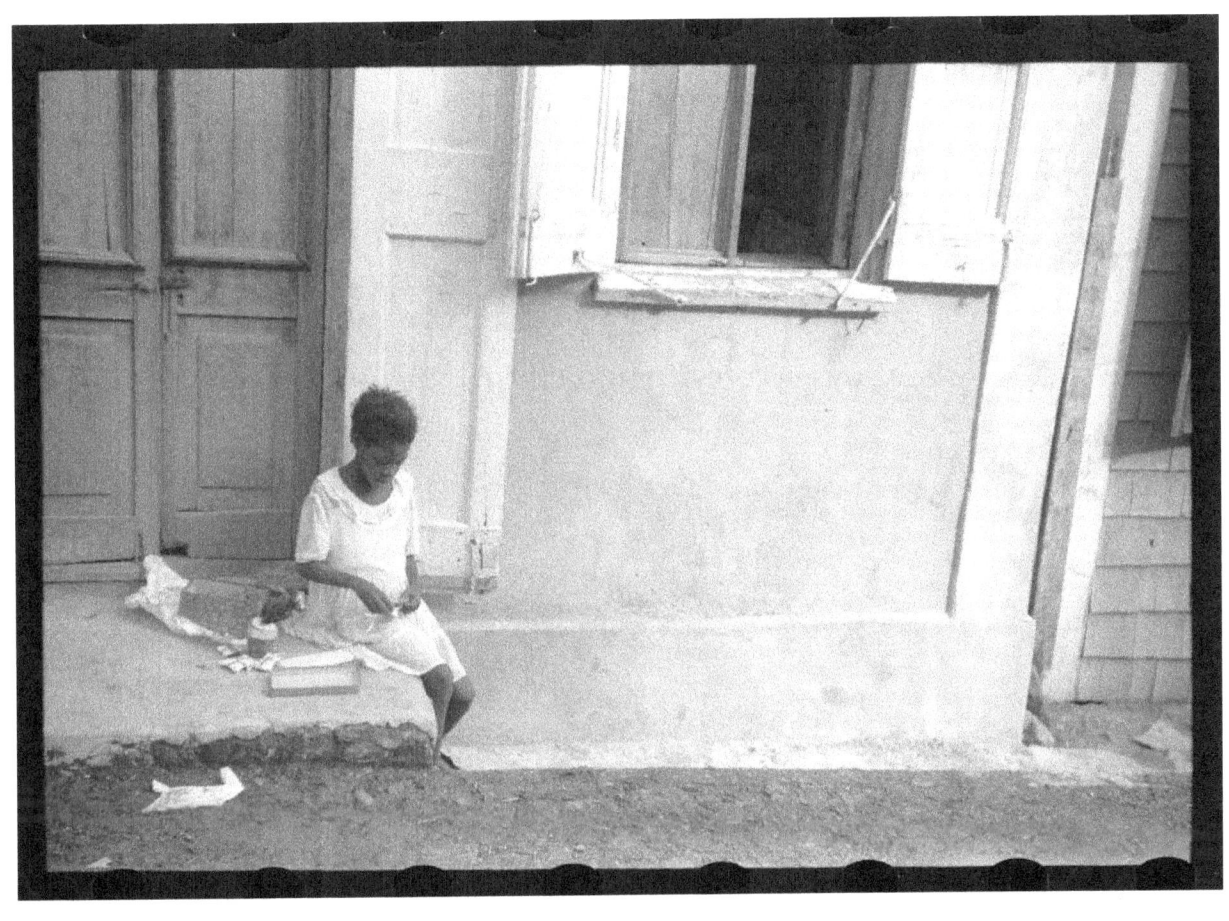

Delano, Jack. "Christmas Trees for Sale at a Gas Station. Woonsocket, Rhode Island." December 1940. Library of Congress.
http://www.loc.gov/pictures/item/2017793038/

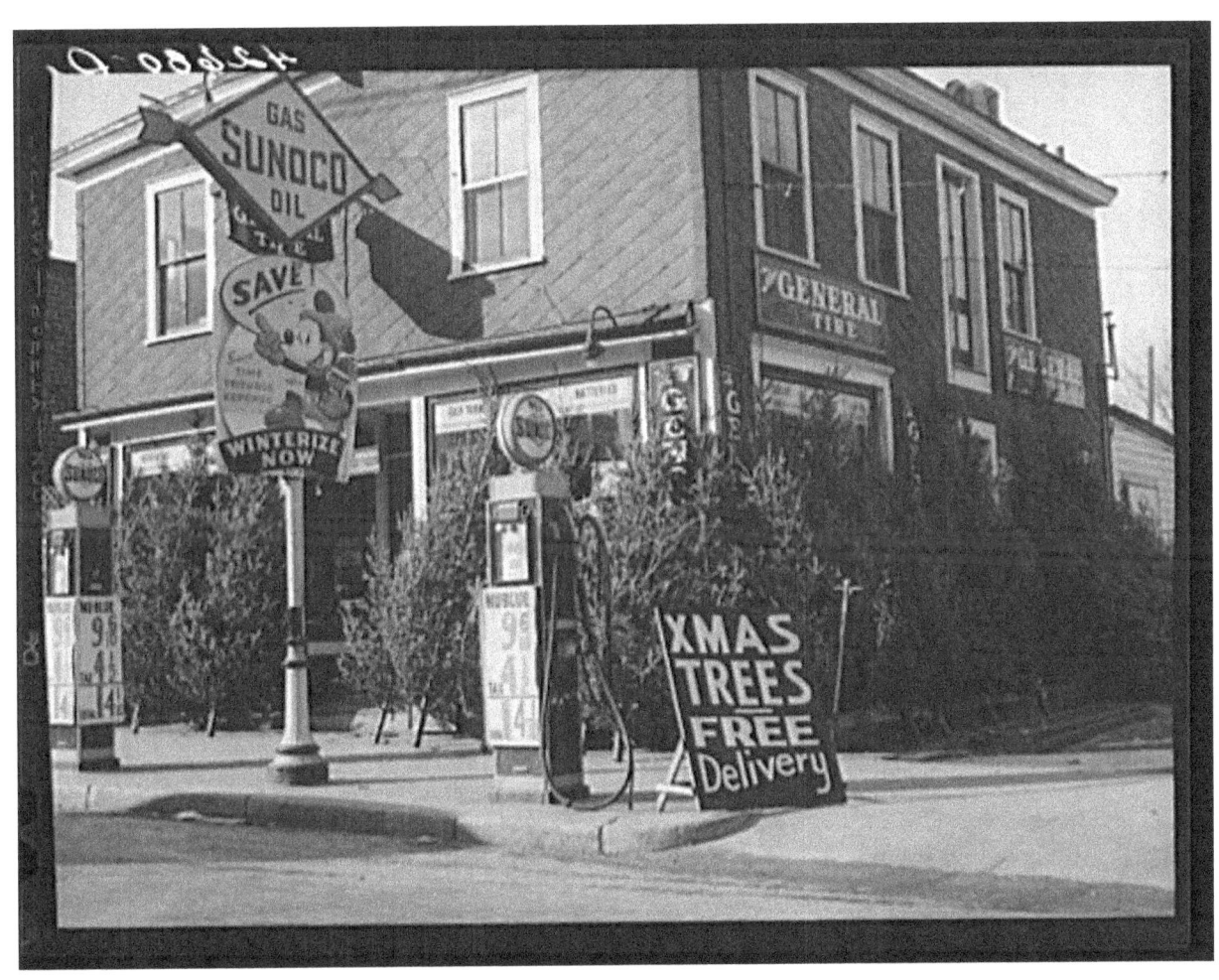

Delano, Jack. "Manuel Andrews, a Portuguese boy near Falmouth, Massachusetts. December 1940. Library of Congress. http://www.loc.gov/pictures/item/2017793261/

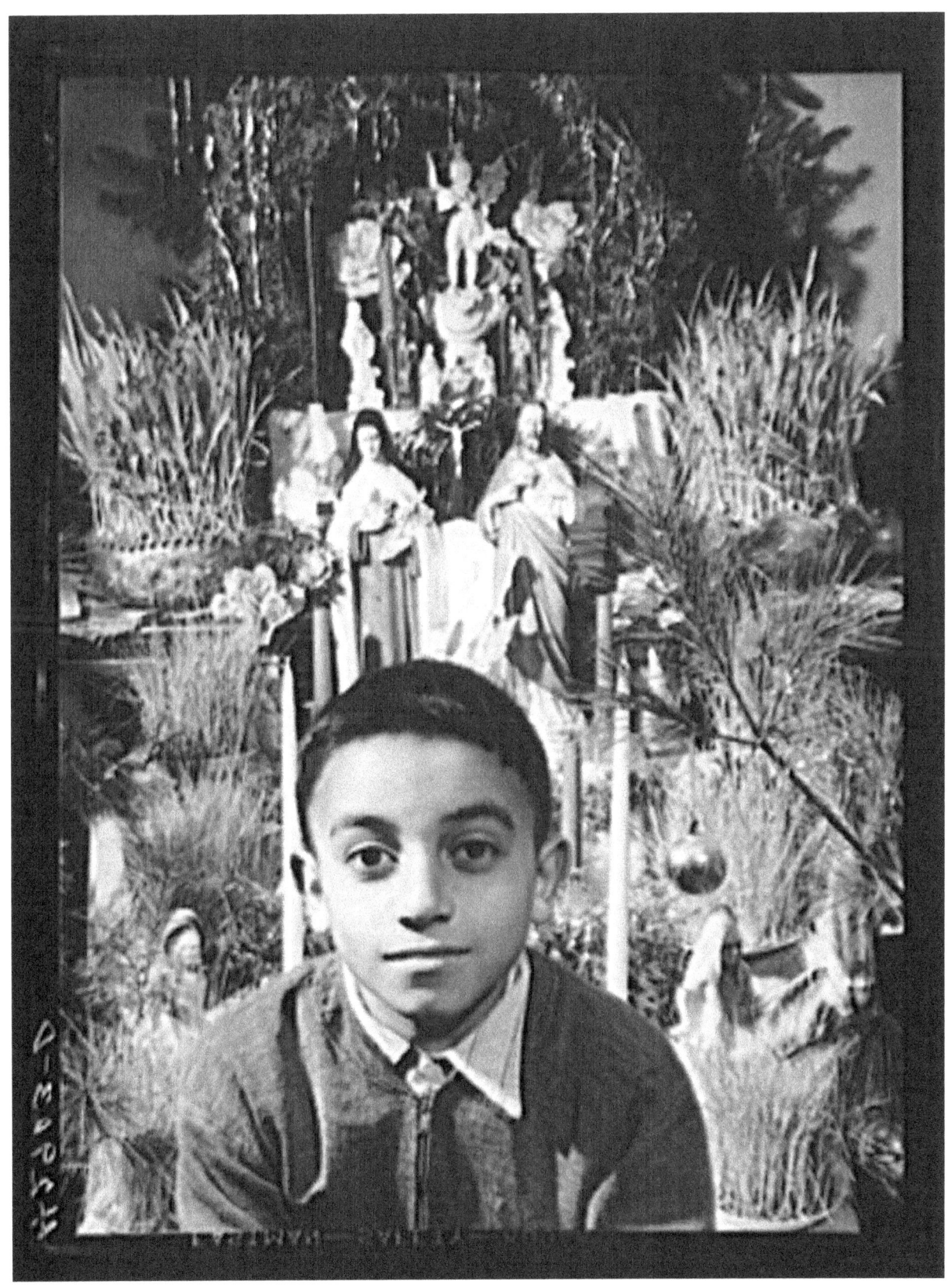

Collier, John, Jr. "Christmas in the Home of a Government Executive, Virginia." December 1941.
http://www.loc.gov/pictures/item/2017821863/

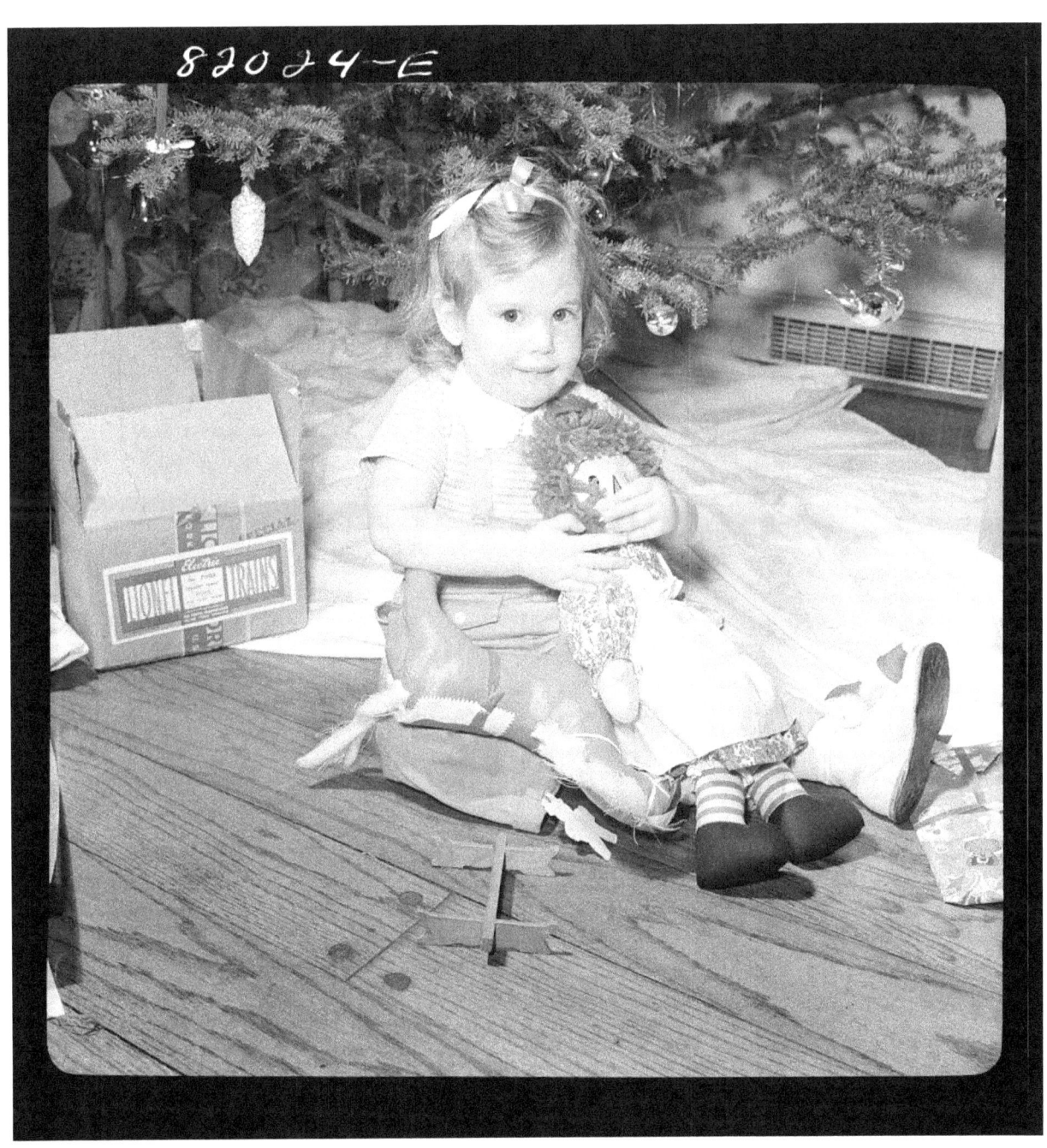

Collins, Marjory. "New York, New York. Toy department display at R. H. Macy and Company department store during the week before Christmas." December 1942. Library of Congress.

http://www.loc.gov/pictures/item/2017841518/

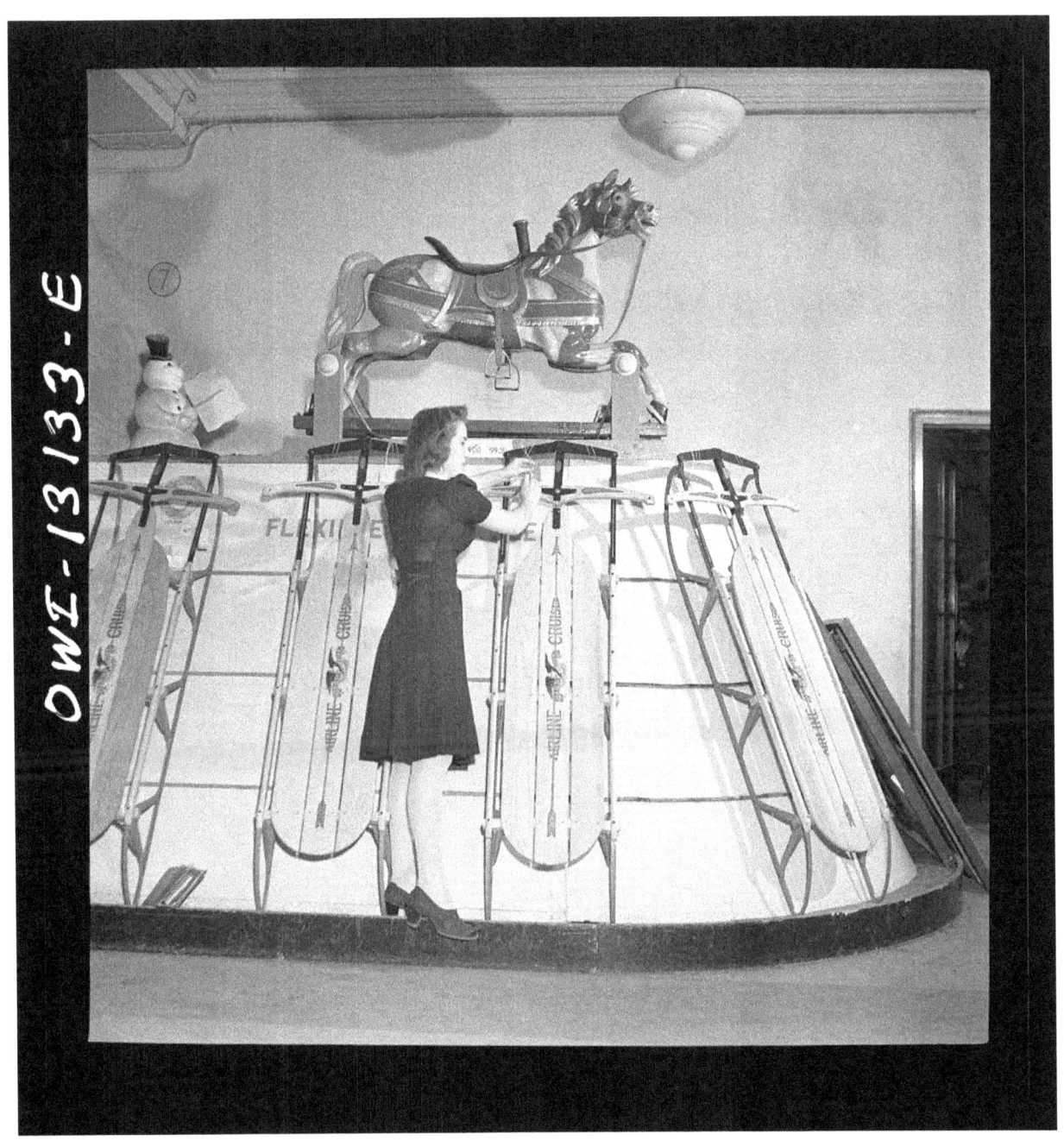

Collins, Marjory. "New York, New York. R. H. Macy and Company department store during the week before Christmas." **December 1942. Library of Congress.** http://www.loc.gov/pictures/item/2017841527/

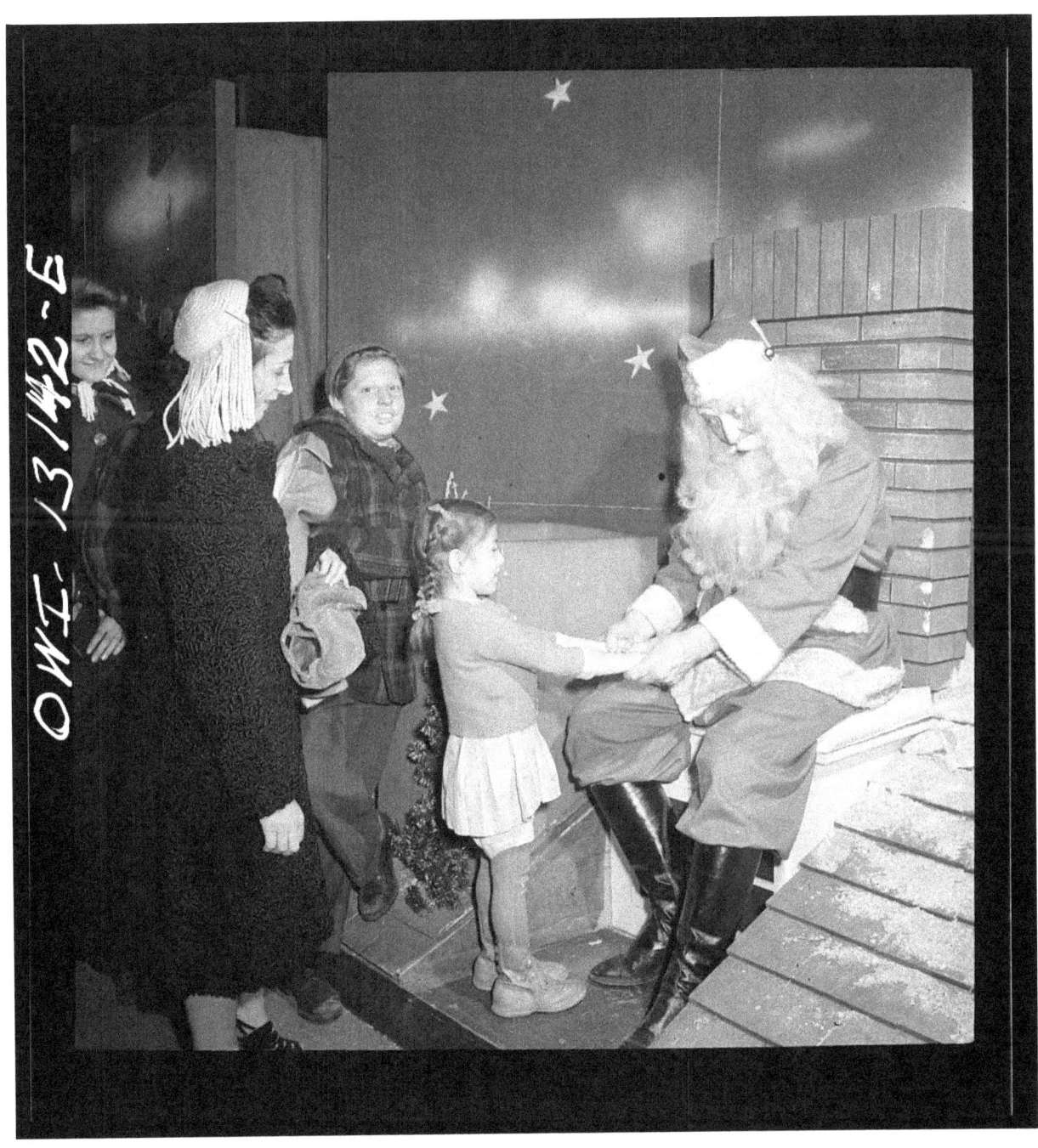

www.ingramcontent.com/pod-product-compliance
Lightning Source LLC
Chambersburg PA
CBHW062334220526
45469CB00008B/2716